LEGAL PATHWAYS TO DEEP DECARBONIZATION IN THE UNITED STATES: SUMMARY AND KEY RECOMMENDATIONS

Michael B. Gerrard and John C. Dernbach

Editors

ENVIRONMENTAL LAW INSTITUTE
Washington, D.C.

1730 M Street NW, Washington, DC 20036

Cover design by Davonne Flanagan.
Artwork by Ivan Pharabod from James H. Williams et al., Pathways to Deep Decarbonization in the United States, U.S. 2050 Report (Deep Decarbonization Pathways Project & Energy and Environmental Economics, Inc., 2015)

Published November 2018.

Printed in the United States of America
ISBN 978-1-58576-195-1

Contents

Contributing Authors

Stephen Oliver Andersen, American Director of Research, Institute for Governance & Sustainable Development

Nathan (BP) Borgford-Parnell, Science Affairs Adviser and Regional Assessment Coordinator, Climate & Clean Air Coalition to Reduce Short-Lived Climate Pollutants

C. Baird Brown, Principal, eco(n)law LLC

Keturah Brown, Associate, Van Ness Feldman LLP

Michael Burger, Executive Director, Sabin Center for Climate Change Law

Andrea Hudson Campbell, Partner, Van Ness Feldman LLP

Federico Cheever (deceased) was Professor of Law at the University of Denver Sturm College of Law

Michael T. Craig, recent Ph.D. recipient, Carnegie Mellon University

John C. Dernbach, Commonwealth Professor of Environmental Law and Sustainability, Widener University Commonwealth Law School

K.K. DuVivier, Professor of Law, University of Denver Sturm College of Law

Steven Ferrey, Professor of Law, Suffolk University Law School

Joshua P. Fershée, Professor of Law, West Virginia University College of Law

Robert L. Fischman, George P. Smith, II Distinguished Professor of Law and Adjunct Professor of Public and Environmental Affairs, Indiana University Maurer School of Law

Robert Freedman, Partner, Shearman & Sterling LLP

Michael B. Gerrard, Andrew Sabin Professor of Professional Practice, Columbia Law School

Ben Haley, Co-Founder, Evolved Energy Research

Stephen Herzenberg, Executive Director, Keystone Research Center

Tracy Hester, Lecturer, University of Houston Law Center

Shi-Ling Hsu, D'Alemberte Professor of Law, Florida State University College of Law

Blake Hudson, A.L. O'Quinn Chair in Environmental Law and Professor of Law, University of Houston Law Center

David Ismay, Senior Attorney, Conservation Law Foundation

Wendy B. Jacobs, Emmett Clinical Professor of Environmental Law and Director, Harvard Law School Emmett Environmental Law & Policy Clinic

Ryan A. Jones, Co-Founder, Evolved Energy Research

Réna Kakon, Legal Counsel, Fenix International (ENGIE Group)

David Kanter, Assistant Professor of Environmental Studies, New York University

Kit Kennedy, Senior Director, Climate and Clean Energy Program, Natural Resources Defense Council

Alexandra B. Klass, Distinguished McKnight University Professor, University of Minnesota Law School

Gabe Kwok, Principal, Evolved Energy Research

Monica Lamb, Clean Energy Lawyer and Advisor

Peter H. Lehner, Senior Strategic Advisor and Senior Attorney, Earthjustice

Gregg P. Macey, Professor of Law, Brooklyn Law School

Gary E. Marchant, Regents' Professor and Lincoln Professor of Emerging Technologies, Law and Ethics, Arizona State University Sandra Day O'Connor College of Law

Caitlin McCoy, Climate, Clean Air & Energy Fellow, Harvard Law School Environmental and Energy Law Program

Robert B. McKinstry, Jr., Environmental and Climate Law Attorney and Consultant

Claire Melvin, Associate Attorney, Shearman & Sterling LLP

Aoife O'Leary, Senior Legal Manager, Environmental Defense Fund

Uma Outka, Professor of Law, University of Kansas School of Law

Lee Paddock, Associate Dean for Environmental Law Studies, The George Washington University Law School

Trip Pollard, Senior Attorney, Southern Environmental Law Center

Melissa Powers, Jeffrey Bain Faculty Scholar and Professor of Law, Lewis & Clark Law School

David A. Repka, Partner (retired), Winston & Strawn LLP

Nathan A. Rosenberg, Adjunct Professor, University of Iowa College of Law

Jim Rossi, Associate Dean for Research and Judge D.L. Lansden Professor of Law, Vanderbilt University Law School

Charles R. Sensiba, Partner, Troutman Sanders LLP

James Charles Smith, John Byrd Martin Chair of Law Emeritus, University of Georgia School of Law

Tyson R. Smith, Nuclear Energy Lawyer and Advisor

Amy L. Stein, Professor of Law and University Term Professor, University of Florida Levin College of Law

Paul C. Stern, President, Social and Environmental Research Institute (USA)

Michael A. Swiger, Partner, Van Ness Feldman LLP

Melinda E. Taylor, Senior Lecturer, University of Texas School of Law, and Academic Director, Kay Bailey Hutchison Center for Energy, Law, and Business

Elizabeth Trujillo, Professor of Law, Texas A&M University School of Law

Michael P. Vandenbergh, David Daniels Allen Distinguished Chair of Law, Vanderbilt University Law School

James M. Van Nostrand, Professor and Director, Center for Energy and Sustainable Development at West Virginia University College of Law

Romany M. Webb, Associate Research Scholar and Senior Fellow, Columbia Law School Sabin Center for Climate Change Law

Steven Weissman, Lecturer, University of California Berkeley Goldman School of Public Policy and Vermont Law School, and Senior Policy Advisor, Center for Sustainable Energy

Jessica Wentz, Senior Fellow and Associate Research Scholar, Columbia Law School Sabin Center for Climate Change Law

Sharon L. White, Of Counsel, Van Ness Feldman LLP

James H. Williams, Associate Professor of Energy Systems Management, University of San Francisco, and Director, Deep Decarbonization Pathways Project for the Sustainable Development Solutions Network

Durwood Zaelke, Founder and President, Institute for Governance and Sustainable Development

Avi B. Zevin, Attorney, Institute for Policy Integrity, New York University School of Law

List of Acronyms

AEA: Atomic Energy Act

AIA: American Institute of Architects

BAT: best available technology

BLM: Bureau of Land Management

BOEM: Bureau of Energy Management

CAA: Clean Air Act

CCS: carbon capture and sequestration

CEQ: Council on Environmental Quality

CES: clean energy standard

CFC: chlorofluorocarbon

CO_2: carbon dioxide

CO_2eq: carbon dioxide equivalent

CRP: Conservation Reserve Program

CSP: Conservation Stewardship Program

DAC: direct air capture

DDPP: Deep Decarbonization Pathways Project

DG: distributed generation

DOE: U.S. Department of Energy

DPF: diesel particulate filter

EERS: energy-efficiency resource standard

EIS: environmental impact statement

EISA: Energy Independence and Security Act

EPA: U.S. Environmental Protection Agency

EPAct 2005: Energy Policy Act of 2005

EPCA: Energy Policy and Conservation Act

EQIP: Environmental Quality Incentives Program

ESA: Endangered Species Act

ETS: emissions trading scheme
EU: European Union
EVs: electric vehicles
FAA: Federal Aviation Administration
FAST: Fixing America's Surface Transportation Act
FCIC: Federal Crop Insurance Corporation
FERC: Federal Energy Regulatory Commission
FHA: Federal Housing Administration
FITs: feed-in tariffs
FONSI: finding of no significant impact
FPA: Federal Power Act
FSA: Farm Service Agency
FWS: U.S. Fish and Wildlife Service
GHG: greenhouse gas
Gt: gigaton
GWP: global warming potential
HCFC: hydrochlorofluorocarbon
HDVs: heavy-duty vehicles
HFC: hydrofluorocarbon
HFCV: hydrogen fuel cell vehicle
ICAO: International Civil Aviation Organization
IMO: International Maritime Organization
IPCC: Intergovernmental Panel on Climate Change
ISO: independent system operator
LCCP: life-cycle climate performance
LCRs: local content requirements
LDVs: light-duty vehicles
LEED: Leadership in Energy and Environmental Design

LFG: landfill gas
LWR: light water reactor
M&V: measurement and verification
MEPS: minimum efficiency performance standards
MMT: million metric tons
MPOs: metropolitan planning organizations
MWh: megawatt hours
NEPA: National Environmental Policy Act
NETs: negative emissions technologies
NGCC: natural gas combined cycle
NHTSA: National Highway Traffic Safety Administration
NPDES: national pollutant discharge elimination system
NRC: Nuclear Regulatory Commission
NRCS: Natural Resources Conservation Service
NSPS: new source performance standards
PAB: private activity bond
PHMSA: Pipeline and Hazardous Materials Safety Administration
PM: particulate matter
PPA: power purchase agreement
PTC: production tax credit
PUC: public utilities commission
PURPA: Public Utility Regulatory Policies Act
PV: photovoltaic
R&D: research and development
RCRA: Resource Conservation and Recovery Act
RD&D: research, development, and demonstration
RFS: Renewable Fuel Standard
RMA: Risk Management Agency (USDA)

RPS: renewable portfolio standard
RTO: regional transmission organization
SFO: Sustainable Finance Organization
SIP: state implementation plan
SMR: small modular reactor
SWPA: Southwestern Power Administration
TNCs: transportation network companies
TOD: transit-oriented development
TPO: third-party ownership
UNFCCC: United Nations Framework Convention on Climate Change
USDA: U.S. Department of Agriculture
VMT: vehicle miles traveled
WAPA: Western Area Power Administration
ZEB: zero-energy building
ZNE: zero net energy

To purchase *Legal Pathways to Deep Decarbonization in the United States,* the longer volume from which the summaries and key recommendations in this shorter book originated, visit www.eli.org/DeepDecarbonization

INTRODUCTION

by John C. Dernbach

This book contains key information and recommendations from a longer volume, *Legal Pathways to Deep Decarbonization in the United States. Legal Pathways* is based on two reports by the Deep Decarbonization Pathways Project (DDPP) that explain technical and policy pathways for reducing U.S. greenhouse gas (GHG) emissions by at least 80% from 1990 levels by 2050. This 80x50 target and similarly aggressive carbon abatement goals are often referred to as deep decarbonization, distinguished because it requires systemic changes to the energy economy.

Using these technical and policy pathways, *Legal Pathways* provides a legal playbook for deep decarbonization in the United States, identifying well over one thousand legal options for enabling the United States to address one of the greatest problems facing this country and the rest of humanity. In North American football, a playbook is a comprehensive listing of all of the plays that can be employed by a particular team. In any one game, some of these plays will be used, and some will not, depending on the circumstances. But coaches for the team draw from the playbook to employ an appropriate combination of plays in order to win. Similarly here, it is not likely that all of the legal pathways will be will be used, but public and private decisionmakers can employ various combinations of these pathways to achieve the needed reductions in U.S. GHG emissions.

Legal Pathways includes a chapter explaining the DDPP reports, and then addresses in detail 34 different topics in as many chapters. These 34 chapters cover energy efficiency, conservation, and fuel switching; electricity decarbonization; fuel decarbonization; carbon capture and negative emissions; non-carbon dioxide climate pollutants, and a variety of cross-cutting issues. Each chapter explains the topic in enough detail to enable readers without a specialized background to understand it, including a discussion of its contribution to U.S. GHG emissions and its potential to reduce such emissions. Each chapter also identifies the main legal issues involved in decarbonization, and describes and explains the main legal options or pathways for successfully addressing these legal issues. These options or pathways involve federal, state, and local law, as well as private governance. (Many of the recommendations that apply to states are also relevant to tribal governments and U.S.

territories.) Authors were asked to include options even if they do not now seem politically realistic or likely; the idea was to identify all significant legal pathways for deep decarbonization in the United States, recognizing that *Legal Pathways* hopefully should have not just immediate value but value over time.

The present volume grows out of a desire to get the main messages of the longer volume to the broadest possible audience. It provides thumbnail summaries of each of the chapters from *Legal Pathways.* It also contains key recommendations from each chapter, the key plays available for deep decarbonization. Finally, an index organizes the key recommendations by actor (e.g., local governments), enabling readers to see in one place all of the key recommendations for any particular actor, regardless of the chapter in which they originated.

While both the scale and complexity of deep decarbonization are enormous, this book has the same simple message as *Legal Pathways*: deep decarbonization is achievable in the United States using laws that exist or could be enacted. These legal tools can be employed with significant economic, social, environmental, and national security benefits.

Part I

CONTEXT

Chapter 1: Technical and Economic Feasibility of Deep Decarbonization in the United States

by James H. Williams, David Ismay, Ryan A. Jones, Gabe Kwok, and Ben Haley

The Deep Decarbonization Pathways Project (DDPP) is an international research collaboration that explores how individual countries can reduce their greenhouse gas (GHG) emissions consistent with limiting global warming to 2° Celsius (C) or less. The term "deep decarbonization" refers to dramatic reductions in carbon dioxide (CO_2) emissions from fossil fuel combustion, which is the primary global challenge in reducing GHG emissions. The DDPP consists of independent research teams from 16 countries who do not necessarily reflect the policy positions of their national governments. From the outset, the DDPP aimed to steer the focus of climate policy away from limited incremental emissions reductions toward the complete transformation of the energy system. To this end, the DDPP teams emphasized an analytical approach that demonstrates why near-term decisions about long-lived infrastructure investments must be made with the ultimate emissions goals in mind.

The chapter starts with a brief background of the DDPP and its influence on subsequent decarbonization studies and climate policy discussions. The remaining sections describe the study conducted for the United States by the U.S. DDPP research team, including the main objectives and research questions, the modeling approach employed, the scenarios explored, and the main findings of the project. These scenarios include a mixed case in which energy efficiency, renewable energy, nuclear power, and carbon capture and sequestration are used to achieve deep decarbonization. The findings include detailed analytical results describing the sector-by-sector transition to deep decarbonization, along with general principles and quantitative benchmarks for deep decarbonization of energy, and mitigation of non-energy and non-CO_2 GHGs. The final sections of the chapter identify key policy challenges and offer recommendations for effective policymaking.

Key Recommendations:

- To successfully achieve deep decarbonization, all levels of government and private actors should engage in integrated planning based on the efficient and transparent sharing of information between stakeholders, many of whom have not historically coordinated their efforts.
- In order to help minimize carbon lock-in and stranded assets, all levels of government and private actors should assess all near-term decisions against long-term goals and viable pathways to achieve them, balancing replacing retiring fossil fuel-based infrastructure with available low-carbon technologies.

Selected Figures From the Deep Decarbonization Pathways Project

Decarbonization Wedges for the United States, Mixed Case Scenario

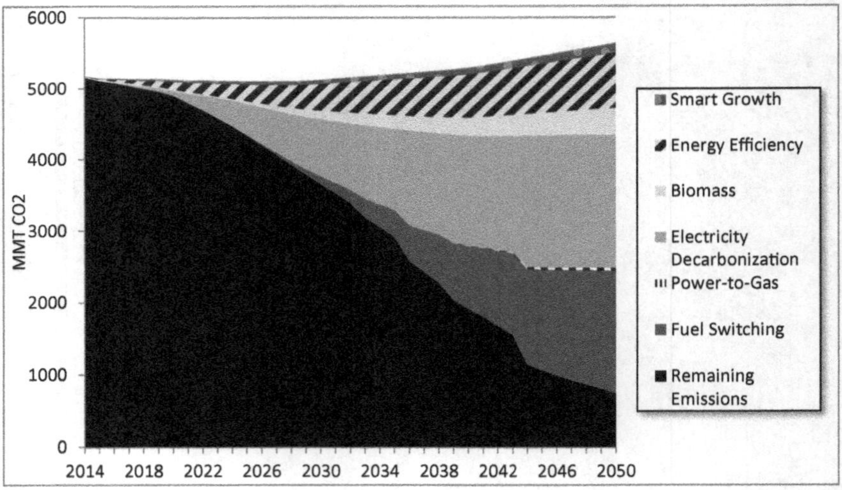

Source: JAMES H. WILLIAMS ET AL., PATHWAYS TO DEEP DECARBONIZATION IN THE UNITED STATES, U.S. 2050 REPORT, VOLUME 1: TECHNICAL REPORT fig. 10 (Deep Decarbonization Pathways Project & Energy and Environmental Economics, Inc., 2015), *available at* http://usddpp.org/downloads/2014-technical-report.pdf.

Mixed Case Electric Sector Supply and Demand

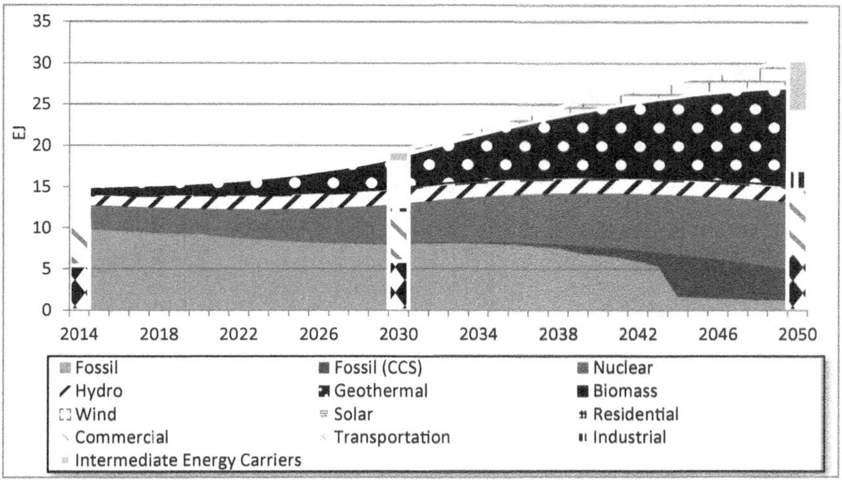

Source: James H. Williams et al., Pathways to Deep Decarbonization in the United States, U.S. 2050 Report, Volume 1: Technical Report fig. 28 (Deep Decarbonization Pathways Project & Energy and Environmental Economics, Inc., 2015), *available at* http://usddpp.org/downloads/2014-technical-report.pdf.

Mixed Case Liquids Supply and Demand

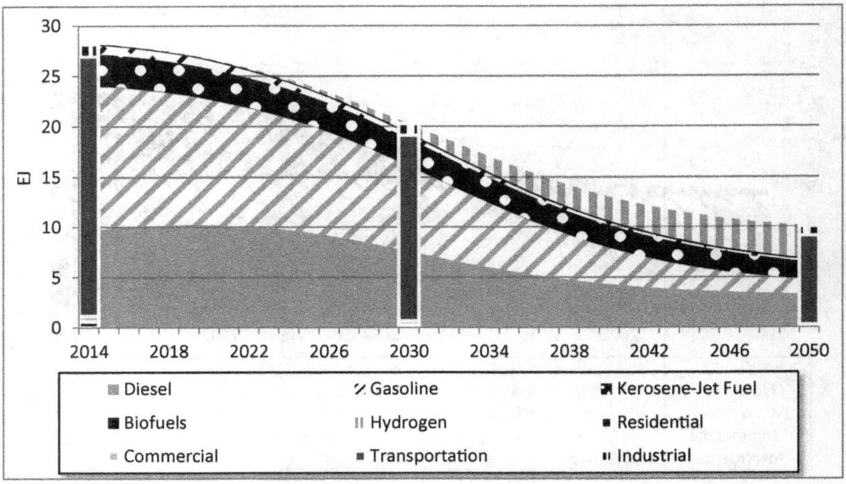

Source: James H. Williams et al., Pathways to Deep Decarbonization in the United States, U.S. 2050 Report, Volume 1: Technical Report fig. 35 (Deep Decarbonization Pathways Project & Energy and Environmental Economics, Inc., 2015), *available at* http://usddpp.org/downloads/2014-technical-report.pdf.

Part II

Cross-Cutting Approaches to Reducing Emissions

Chapter 2: Carbon Pricing

by Shi-Ling Hsu

Carbon pricing is commonly meant to refer to two main types of climate policy instruments: carbon taxation and cap-and-trade programs. Although a number of economic and technological uncertainties render it difficult to estimate the amount of emissions reductions that can be achieved by a carbon pricing scheme, a carbon pricing scheme must be a foundational part of any effective climate policy. The chapter therefore discusses the legal issues that arise in connection with carbon pricing schemes. Because of its ubiquity and breadth, and because of its capacity to effect fairly large economic changes, a carbon pricing law should enjoy broad political support and, in most democratic countries, explicit legislative authorization. Further, the additional implementation issues involved with establishing a cap-and-trade program require some additional legal planning. For example, many cap-and-trade programs provide for the issuance of offsets, permits created above and beyond the initially established "cap," by the approval of some project deemed to have somehow reduced emissions. While useful, offsets have proven to be problematic, sometimes rewarding clever emissions accounting rather than actual reductions. Carbon taxation, however, usually involves fewer moving administrative parts, and thus fewer legal issues. As between the two, carbon taxation is less administratively complicated, and the better starting point for climate policy. The chapter describes one carbon tax option to serve as a policy foundation upon which other policies could be added, such as traditional emissions regulations under the Clean Air Act (CAA), if needed. The chapter also looks at the legal issues surrounding how a carbon tax would be designed and implemented.

Key Recommendation:

- Congress should consider adopting a carbon tax that begins at $25 per metric ton, increases over time based on rising damage from climate change, and the revenues from which are spent for some combination of economic efficiency, income redistribution, and climate policy purposes.

Chapter 3: Behavior

by Michael P. Vandenbergh and Paul C. Stern

The chapter asks why household behavior matters for deep decarbonization, and how laws, policies, and programs that target behavior change can be employed to facilitate decarbonization. The pathways set forth in the DDPP reports all presume widespread public acceptance of new policies, as well as changes in household actions that directly affect carbon emissions, mainly via consumer adoption of technologies that have lower GHG footprints. While none of the DDPP pathways relies on explicit behavior change interventions to achieve emissions reductions, behavior change remains central to the project: the demand for energy services and uptake and use of technologies that reduce carbon emissions, particularly in the domains of energy efficiency and renewable energy, require massive amounts of behavior change between now and 2050. Because factors affecting individual and household behavior differ per behavioral type, interventions need to be tailored to specific behaviors. It is also important to recognize that public and private initiatives both play a role in driving the kinds of behavior change necessary to achieve deep decarbonization. The best available research indicates that achieving the rates of adoption included in the DDPP pathways is indeed feasible; however, this will require more than policies that require change or make adoption financially attractive. The most realistic analysis of the potential for change must consider the technical potential for change, the behavioral plasticity, and the policy plasticity (or feasibility) of adopting and implementing the best-known interventions.

Key Recommendations:

- Federal, state, and local governments, in addition to corporations and other private organizations, should adopt and implement specific strategies for improving energy efficiency in buildings, focused on:
  - » increasing the uptake of energy-efficient buildings, including via energy audits of existing homes and energy rating systems for new homes
  - » increasing the uptake of more energy-efficient home equipment, including green leases and improved life-cycle cost information for retailers and householders.

- Federal, state, and local governments, in addition to corporations and other private organizations, should further use, test, and evaluate specific strategies to reduce carbon emissions from the operation of existing and new home equipment and buildings, including provision of monthly feedback and implementation of information campaigns.
- Federal, state, and local governments, in addition to corporations and other private organizations, should further use, test, and evaluate specific strategies for reducing carbon emissions from motor vehicles, focused on:
    - » increasing motor vehicle efficiency, including improved energy labeling and vehicle fleet buyers' use of supply chain pressure
    - » further use, testing, and evaluation of strategies for reducing carbon emissions from the operation of existing and new motor vehicles and other forms of transportation, including provision of immediate fuel use feedback devices and development of eco-driving education programs.
- Federal, state, and local governments, in addition to corporations and other private organizations, should consider using specific strategies to increase adoption of household-level renewable energy systems and purchases of products with low life-cycle emissions, such as informal marketing through neighborhoods and social networks and targeted marketing to environmentally minded consumers.
- Federal, state, and local governments should adopt and implement policy measures to reduce demand for energy services, not just to reduce the energy needed to supply those services.
- Federal, state, and local governments, in addition to private-sector decisionmakers, should address generational-scale lifestyle changes in two ways: playing offense, particularly when policymakers confront forks in the road where some lifestyle shifts could facilitate deep decarbonization, and playing defense by heading off lifestyle shifts that could undermine deep decarbonization.

Chapter 4: Technological Innovation

by Gary E. Marchant

Deep decarbonization will require the widespread and relatively rapid deployment of clean technologies that are consistent with a deep decarbonization pathway. Market forces, including the potential for cost savings from energy efficiency, corporate responsibility programs, and public relations, will provide some incentives for adoption of cleaner technologies, but will be insufficient to drive adoption of decarbonization technologies as broadly and as quickly as needed. Accordingly, legal interventions will be needed to force adoption of decarbonization technologies at the level and pace needed to prevent unacceptable climate change harm. The chapter addresses the choice, implications, and coordination of legal interventions needed to meet deep decarbonization goals, focusing on the United States. There are a number of possible legal interventions available to encourage technologies consistent with deep decarbonization, but none alone are sufficient to achieve the deep cuts needed in carbon emissions set forth in deep decarbonization pathways. Therefore, a portfolio of different legal tools will be needed, and must be coordinated to ensure an integrated effort.

Key Recommendations:

- If federal agencies, such as the U.S. Environmental Protection Agency (EPA), National Highway Traffic Safety Administration (NHTSA), and U.S. Department of Energy (DOE), that adopt and enforce regulatory standards responsible for reducing GHG emissions seek to achieve the deep decarbonization targets, they should adopt, review, and revise such standards as appropriate to ensure they are consistent and synergistic with deep decarbonization pathways.
- The federal government should provide expedited regulatory approval pathways for some clean technologies, but take care to minimize the risk that such "short cuts" ignore unintended effects or preclude public input.
- Congress should adopt an appropriate carbon tax as the centerpiece of a comprehensive and coordinated strategy to meet deep decarbonization

pathways, and set the level high enough to incentivize the deployment of clean technologies.

- The federal government should provide direct funding of research and development (R&D) for carbon reduction technologies.
- Congress should induce higher levels of R&D in the private sector through an R&D tax credit for carbon reduction technologies.
- The federal government should provide subsidies for clean energy technologies and remove current subsidies for fossil fuels and other unsustainable activities and products.
- The federal government should consider a rejuvenated and focused green patenting program for decarbonization technologies.
- The federal government should consider government-funded competitions and prizes to incentivize low-carbon technologies in addition to or instead of traditional research grants or contracts.
- Congress should put in place a strategy for inducing technological innovation for decarbonization, or authorize an existing or new entity within the federal government to perform this function.
- The federal, state, and local governments, as well as corporations and businesses, should coordinate their efforts to carefully plan technological change inducement programs.

Chapter 5: Financing Large-Scale Projects

by Robert Freedman, Monica Lamb, and Claire Melvin

Development and widespread implementation of carbon-reducing energy solutions at the level necessary to significantly reduce GHG emissions in the United States will require substantial capital investment. However, certain obstacles continue to hold back investment in carbon-reducing energy systems at utility-scale and consumer levels, including: (1) high up-front capital costs; (2) technology risk; (3) energy generation variability and integration costs; (4) tax incentive limitations; (5) location restrictions for consumer investors; (6) burdensome development and permitting time lines; and (7) inadequate transmission infrastructure. Policy changes at the federal, state, and local levels can be used to attract increased investment to carbon-reducing energy solutions and create a dynamic clean energy economy while reducing negative impacts on the climate and environment. Some ways to overcome the challenges described above include: (1) tax incentives, carbon pricing, and financial innovation to reduce high up-front costs and attract a broader investor base; (2) financial protections to reduce risks associated with adopting new technology; (3) adaptable use of the electric grid to address energy generation variability; (4) virtual net metering and community solar to tap into investment from residential and commercial investors otherwise limited by the location and type of property they own or rent; (5) streamlined permitting processes to reduce risks associated with lengthy development time lines; and (6) investments in transmission infrastructure to best take advantage of low- or no-carbon energy resources. The chapter provides an overview of the challenges to attracting capital to carbon-reducing energy projects and the corresponding pathways to overcome such challenges. These pathways will reduce investor risk and increase investor returns, paving the way for increased investment in the carbon-reducing energy systems that are essential to achieving the necessary levels of decarbonization.

Key Recommendations:

- The federal and state governments should work together with the private sector to study and understand the effects that incentives like the production tax credit (PTC) have on the growth of renewable technologies.

- Assuming that the PTC will not continue past its phaseout date, the federal and state governments should assess the need for new incentives, similar to a PTC, which would permit continued growth for renewable technologies.
- The federal and state governments should work with the private sector to continually assess and adjust incentives like the investment tax credit in order to promote the advancement of new technologies.
- State legislatures should adopt long-term tax incentives that take into account the life of carbon-reducing energy projects in order to allow stakeholders to plan investments and growth for the future.
- Congress and federal agencies should consider adopting loan programs similar to the Advanced Technology Vehicles Manufacturing Loan Program that are aimed at the development of more-efficient renewable energy production.
- The federal, state, and local governments should support financing of carbon reducing technologies through the issuance of green bonds.
- More state and local governments should assess the benefits of a comprehensive renewable energy plan that takes into account multiple stakeholders (i.e., cost to consumer, grid integration, and private investment).
- Congress should expand the pool of investors that can claim the tax incentives for investments in renewable energy generation by offering tax incentives in the form of cash grants.
- States should consider adopting and implementing programs similar to Texas' "competitive renewable energy zones" program that are directed at improving and expanding transmission infrastructure.

Chapter 6: Financing at the Grid Edge

by C. Baird Brown

The chapter discusses legal impediments and solutions for customer, community, and third-party financing of behind-the-meter and community-scale clean generation, storage, and energy efficiency. Current levels of investment by utilities and independent power producers fall well below levels needed to meet deep decarbonization goals. Investments at the "grid edge" driven by customers and communities not only contribute to clean energy goals, but also reduce energy prices and improve the resilience of the power supply. These linked incentives can help attract the new investment we need. To unleash investment at the grid edge, legal reforms are needed to permit ownership of local energy resources and sales of energy and other services by customers, communities, and their local suppliers; to encourage utilities and regional transmission organizations (RTOs) to foster transparent markets for services from grid-edge resources and make direct purchases of such services; to provide better information on the usage of customers and the needs of the grid; and to adapt and reuse existing finance markets and create new institutions that support grid-edge finance. These reforms will permit customers and communities to structure creditworthy projects that qualify for financing.

Key Recommendations:

- States should assure that each energy customer:
  - » may generate and manage energy behind its meter and contract with third parties to assist them in doing so;
  - » may purchase clean energy from local energy providers through its own or the provider's distribution system;
  - » may purchase energy through local group or community arrangements;
  - » is entitled to prompt, convenient access to all information gathered by public utilities regarding its own energy use and energy services it delivers; and

» is entitled to grid access on a nondiscriminatory basis to provide wholesale energy and energy services to the local distribution company through open, transparent markets or at just and reasonable rates.

- States should assure that each community:
  » may purchase or generate energy on behalf of its citizens directly or through contractual arrangements with third parties;

  » is entitled to prompt, convenient access to aggregate information gathered by public utilities about their citizens' energy use and the energy services the citizens deliver; and

  » is entitled to act as an aggregator of energy and energy services provided by its citizens with the same rights to deliver wholesale energy and energy services as its citizens.
- The Federal Energy Regulatory Commission (FERC) should continue to work toward "market participation models" that take account of the specific characteristics of grid-edge resources so that they have access on a nondiscriminatory basis to provide wholesale energy and energy services in the RTO markets.
- FERC could require the establishment of RTOs throughout the country.
- State utility commissions should require utility planning that identifies locations on the utility distribution systems where location of grid-edge resources can avoid the need for additional distribution assets, and should encourage utilities to engage in "utility-private partnerships" to procure services from grid-edge resources.
- State utility commissions should promote a utility business model that provides new sources of revenue and profit consistent with encouraging the growth of grid-edge resources; the business model should include decoupling mechanisms so that utilities do not receive income in excess of their revenue requirement plus earned incentives, with the result that megawatt hours (MWh) of sales do not drive profits.
- Congress should impose a uniform carbon price on all energy suppliers to give decarbonization investments at the grid edge a competitive advantage without distorting markets.

- Building industry stakeholders should promote verifiable standards for new building energy efficiency, ensure that construction and real estate sales contracts for new buildings require testing and verification of energy performance, and require building appraisals and mortgage credit evaluations to reflect building energy consumption.
- States and larger localities or regions should establish green banks or similar Sustainable Finance Organizations (SFOs).
- Congress should establish an agency that can purchase loans and issue asset-backed securities for residential and small business energy-efficiency and renewable energy loans and provide credit support for clean energy lending, including through SFOs.
- Wherever any governmental agency has jurisdiction over an energy project participant, it should use its authority to require measurement and verification (M&V) metering and data collection devices that permit accurate measurement of energy savings and carbon performance from energy-efficiency projects and public reporting of carbon performance information on an ongoing basis.
- Congress and state legislatures should act to allow low-income energy subsidy funds to be combined with private finance to create low-income housing rehabilitation programs that require energy-efficiency standards be met in the rehabilitation process.

Chapter 7: Materials Consumption and Solid Waste

by Michael Burger

The circular economy represents a powerful new paradigm for materials consumption and solid waste management. Instead of beginning with extraction and ending with waste, the circular economy begins with material already in use, or else material designed for iterative uses, moves through production and consumption, and into waste management, which secures a revived or altered source material, which in turn moves though production and consumption, and so on, over and over again. Achieving significant GHG reductions in this area requires widespread shifts in production and consumption toward what can be expressed succinctly in a familiar refrain: "reduce, reuse, recycle." There are a number of legal pathways to achieving emissions reductions through materials consumption and solid waste management. Corporate governance as well as R&D of new materials can play a significant role, and significant advances can be made through regulatory interventions.

Key Recommendations:

- Congress could pass legislation that sets forth minimum recycled content requirements for a wide range of materials and products.
- Congress could pass legislation that establishes extended producer responsibility for a wide range of products.
- Congress could pass legislation that establishes life-cycle assessment and disclosure requirements for a wide range of materials and products.
- Congress could pass legislation that establishes minimum state recycling rates and food scrap diversion rates.
- Congress could pass legislation that establishes procurement requirements for the federal government consistent with circular economy and deep decarbonization goals.
- Congress could pass legislation that funds R&D into alternative biomaterials that can substitute for plastics.

- States should adopt laws that other states have adopted on the waste problems posed by products, packaging, food scraps, and industrial waste.
- Local governments should adopt laws that other local governments have adopted on the waste problems posed by products, packaging, food scraps, and industrial waste.
- State and local governments could adopt laws with more ambitious goals (e.g., zero waste), intermediate targets and timetables for achieving these more ambitious goals, and means of achieving them.
- Companies that operate at every stage of economic activity—from extraction to transportation to manufacture to retail to service—should consider mechanisms, including circular economy concepts, through which they can demonstrate leadership in materials and solid waste management and reduce the use and waste of embedded GHG emissions.

Chapter 8: International Trade

by Elizabeth Trujillo

As countries fulfill their commitments to the Paris Climate Agreement and engage in climate change mitigation policies and domestic decarbonization strategies, governments must ensure their policies comply with their trade obligations. The chapter provides a brief overview of key areas where international trade rules may impact U.S. policies geared toward decarbonization. It focuses primarily on the policies needed for decarbonization, as outlined in the DDPP reports, that are connected to international trade rules, with the goal of finding ways of using the international trade legal framework as another tool for encouraging, rather than inhibiting, decarbonization efforts at the national level. Part II sets out the policy tools promoting decarbonization most likely to implicate or conflict with trade rules. Part III provides a primer on the main trade rules that intersect with decarbonization tools, such as border tax adjustments, subsidies, labeling schemes, and local content requirements (LCRs). Part IV examines specific cases where decarbonization has led to trade law conflicts as well as recommendations for decarbonization strategies that are trade compliant and avoid such conflicts in the future. Part V considers preferential trade agreements as an alternative way that trade policymakers and regulators may work together toward decarbonization.

Key Recommendations

- State and local governments must adopt decarbonization laws that comply with international trade rules.
- If Congress adopts decarbonization laws, they must comply with international trade rules.
- State and local governments should avoid adopting decarbonization laws that contain LCRs.
- Congress and state legislatures should continue to use subsidies (preferably without LCRs) in the form of tax credits, accelerated depreciation, or cash grants, in combination with other incentives, to help create a market for renewable energy that would eventually drive down some of the production costs.

- If federal, state, or local governments design a decarbonization law that contains LCRs, it should meet the national treatment requirements under Article III of the General Agreement on Tariffs and Trade.
- If Congress or state or local legislatures decide to adopt an LCR for decarbonization, they could limit the LCR to government procurement, particularly if it is linked to decarbonization policies or protection of public health.
- The U.S. Department of State should play a lead role in addressing border tax adjustments and other decarbonization strategies within the negotiation phase of preferential trade agreements, particularly regional and plurilateral agreements.
- The U.S. government as well as state governments should consider feed-in tariffs (FITs) as long as they comply with applicable trade rules.
- Congress and states should structure decarbonization labeling schemes so as not to discriminate against foreign imports.
- The U.S. Department of State should take a lead role in negotiating multilateral agreements concerning climate change that include decarbonization labeling standards.
- The U.S. Department of State and U.S. Trade Representative should further a (preferably federal) decarbonization strategy tied to climate change mitigation and clean energy strategies when negotiating preferential trade agreements.

Part III

Energy Efficiency, Conservation, and Fuel Switching in Buildings and Industry

Chapter 9: Lighting, Appliances, and Other Equipment

by Kit Kennedy

The DDPP reports call for major increases in building and equipment efficiency to reduce U.S. GHG emissions by at least 80 percent from 1990 levels by 2050. While the DOE efficiency standards program is one of the most successful U.S. energy-efficiency policies in driving energy savings, carbon reductions, and consumer savings, it will need to be made even stronger, and an integrated suite of additional and more ambitious energy-efficiency laws and regulations at the federal, state, and local level will be needed to meet the deep decarbonization challenge. Additional action from private actors, such as utilities and businesses, will also be necessary to drive energy-efficiency investments. The chapter discusses the various legal and policy pathways at the federal, state, and local levels to ensure that the energy efficiency of residential, commercial, and industrial products continues to improve at the scale and speed necessary to meet this "80% by 2050" goal.

Key Recommendations:

- Congress, DOE, the Executive Branch, states, and cities should develop an integrated suite of policies that combine, coordinate, and synthesize a full suite of carbon reduction policies with complementary energy efficiency policies, including mandatory minimum energy efficiency standards, voluntary labeling and incentive programs that further increase produce energy efficiency levels over time, tax incentives, and other complementary energy efficiency policies that are part of a larger set of decarbonization policies.
- Congress should enact legislation to create an ambitious federal energy-efficiency resource standard (EERS), which would be a national energy-efficiency goal for electric and natural gas utilities.
- Congress should expand funding and ensure full implementation of key federal low-income energy programs, including the Low Income Home Energy Assistance Program and the Weatherization Assistance Program.

- Congress should amend the Energy Policy and Conservation Ac (EPCA) in order to broaden DOE's authority under EPCA to establish energy efficiency standards for new products; authorize DOE to adopt energy efficiency standards with multiple efficiency metrics; give DOE discretion to establish shorter compliance lead times for energy efficiency standards; and allow for shorter compliance lead times for standards.
- Congress should approve budgets for DOE's Appliance Standards and Building Codes program at a level sufficient to support the staff and resources needed to complete required energy efficiency rulemakings on time.
- DOE should continue and enhance coordination with the DOE energy efficiency standards program and the EPA ENERGY STAR® program. As part of this coordination, ENERGY STAR® product ratings should be updated frequently so that voluntary ENERGY STAR® ratings can increase market penetration for efficient products, helping to give rise to stronger mandatory DOE energy efficiency standards over time. EPA should also consider developing a tiered system for ENERGY STAR® ratings that distinguishes the most efficient products.
- States should adopt an EERS set at an initial ambitious level and periodically reexamine and strengthen the savings level as more-efficient technologies evolve, and should also adopt appropriate policies to align utility business models with energy efficiency investments, make utilities whole for energy efficiency programs, and provide incentives for strong energy efficiency performance.
- States should adopt state energy efficiency standards legislation, seeking waivers from federal preemption when needed, and establish programs that encourage the use of the most energy-efficient appliances and equipment through tax policy, financial incentives, labeling programs, and financing policies.
- Cities should should adopt and fully enforce strong city building energy-efficiency codes; establish city tax deductions or credits for the purchase of energy-efficient equipment; establish financing programs for energy efficiency; and adopt energy efficiency benchmarking ordinances as well as energy audit and energy savings implementation measures.

- Corporations should create sustainability programs headed by high level management that commit them to reduce GHG emissions by at least 25%, improving energy efficiency of operations by at least 50%, and reducing electricity demand by at least 15%.

Chapter 10: New Buildings

by Lee Paddock and Caitlin McCoy

New buildings constructed today can be expected to remain in use until well beyond 2050. As a result, thoughtful decisions now can have a significant impact on reducing the carbon footprint of buildings for decades to come rather than locking in carbon emissions that will make it difficult to achieve the DDPP goals for carbon reduction. Buildings use about 40% of energy produced in the United States and are responsible for about 30% of the nation's CO_2 emissions, making carbon emissions from buildings a priority for carbon reduction. Fortunately, substantial progress has been made in making new buildings more energy efficient, and the technology that would allow for major additional reductions is available. While this progress is important, much more needs to be done in the new building sector to reach the DDPP goals for carbon reduction. The chapter discusses the changes that need to occur and sets out recommendations to help accomplish the carbon reduction goals.

Key Recommendations:

- Federal agencies should fully implement the requirement in the Energy Independence and Security Act (EISA) that federal buildings reduce fossil fuel use by 100% by 2030 measured against a 2003 benchmark, and meet the goal that all new commercial buildings achieve zero net energy (ZNE) by 2030.
- DOE should continue setting leading-edge energy-efficiency standards for heating, cooling, lighting, and other energy-consuming equipment used in new buildings.
- State legislatures should adopt a price for carbon either through a carbon tax or through cap-and-trade systems that include new buildings.
- State legislatures should follow the lead of states like California, Hawaii, and Washington in developing advanced building and energy codes that significantly reduce the energy used by new buildings.
- State legislatures should maintain or adopt laws such as renewable portfolio standards (RPSs), net metering, cost of solar tariffs, and renewable energy tax credits that encourage more rapid integration of renewable

energy into the grid, thereby facilitating the goal of low-carbon electrification of new buildings.

- State legislatures or governors should establish state zero-energy building (ZEB) goals, such as California's goals under California's Building Energy Efficiency Standards.
- State education agencies should provide training opportunities to builders, architects, developers, and others through community colleges, universities, vocational technical schools, and other educational institutions on high-efficiency and ZEB construction practices, as well as passive solar techniques.
- Within the authority granted to them under state law and state building code requirements, local legislative bodies should adopt advanced building and energy codes that drive down carbon use in buildings.
- Local legislative bodies should require energy use disclosures for larger commercial buildings (e.g., buildings larger than 50,000 square feet and multifamily buildings), and require benchmarking information to be made publicly available in a format that is easy to understand so that it can be readily used in rental and purchase decisions.
- Consistent with the 2030 Challenge issued by the American Institute of Architects (AIA), building developers and purchasers should commit to building only ZEBs by no later than 2030.
- Building owners should take full life-cycle costs and the carbon impacts of materials into account when deciding on the energy-efficiency measures for new buildings, with the aim of reducing embodied carbon and overall environmental impacts.

Chapter 11: Existing Buildings

by James Charles Smith

Existing buildings account for 75% of U.S. electricity consumption. The DDPP reports call for a drastic reduction of GHG emissions attributable to buildings, ranging from 87% to 96% depending upon the scenario. Because buildings have long useful lives, the only way to achieve the goal is to retrofit a majority of our existing buildings. The chapter discusses six legal pathways that, when used in combination, may accomplish the objective: energy audits; mandatory retrofit laws; energy-efficiency performance standards for new buildings; voluntary certification systems; switching from fossils fuels to low-carbon electricity; and financing programs.

Key Recommendations:

- Congress should consider requiring an energy audit upon the sale or rental of existing homes and commercial properties, and states should require such an audit if the federal government fails to do so.
- Electric utilities should adopt or expand voluntary home energy audit programs.
- Congress should consider adopting mandatory retrofit laws for energy conservation and decarbonization in existing commercial and residential buildings, and state legislatures should adopt such laws if the federal government fails to do so.
- Congress should consider legislation requiring that all federal buildings, regardless of age, have no fossil fuel-generated energy consumption on or before 2050.
- State public utility commissions could adopt regulations to ensure that all customers receive information on the costs and benefits of switching to electricity.
- Congress should consider enacting laws requiring that building owners who presently use fossil fuel for space and water heating must retrofit their buildings by electrification, and states should enact such laws if a federal mandatory law is not obtainable.

- The Federal Housing Administration (FHA) should launch a pilot program to facilitate the making of energy-efficient mortgages and rehabilitation mortgages at interest rates below the market rate for standard home mortgage loans.

Chapter 12: Industrial Sector

by Gregg P. Macey

Carbon mitigation programs face several contradictions as they turn to the industrial sector. While the Intergovernmental Panel on Climate Change (IPCC) points to industry as a high-carbon pollutant end-use sector, it is already efficient in some respects. This is a product of dozens if not hundreds of years of improvement in motors and heat and steam production. Industry plays a declining role in the United States in terms of energy use. Yet industrial carbon emissions reductions must mirror deep decarbonization goals that are set for other sectors in order to hold global average temperature increases within 2°C. And while there are hundreds of cost-effective energy-efficiency measures that manufacturing subsectors such as iron and steel and cement and lime could adopt, firms often ignore them. These challenges demand a diverse array of legal and policy responses. The chapter outlines a suite of legal pathways that must be pursued in concert to achieve massive carbon emissions reductions across key energy-intensive industries in the United States.

Key Recommendations:

- Congress and the administration should pursue policies that promote efficient end use in the industrial sector, energy supply strategies such as electricity supply decarbonization, fuel switching, material efficiency, and carbon management.
- Congress and the administration should pursue a diverse portfolio of legal tools, including:
  - » carbon pricing;
  - » ad hoc or comprehensive regulatory regimes where a carbon price is set through market mechanisms that respond to emissions standards;
  - » subsidies that target emissions at the high and low ends of the carbon emissions abatement cost curve;
  - » a sectoral crediting mechanism for beyond best available technology (BAT) emissions reductions;

- » improved federal motor and boiler minimum efficiency performance standards (MEPS) to address cross-sector leakage in national emissions trading;
- » harmonized state equipment efficiency standards that are not addressed by federal mandate;
- » and a regulatory floor to encourage material efficiency.

- Congress and the administration should promote available and near-term BAT to shore up the process efficiency of major industrial sectors and lower direct carbon emissions.
- Congress and the administration should focus on key processes that take place within energy-intensive industries, such as fractional distillation in refineries; steam cracking in petrochemical plants; pulp making, drying, and finishing in paper production; preservation, process heating, and machine-driven end uses in food processing; upstream production approaches in the iron and steel sector; conversion of bauxite to alumina and its electrolysis; clinker production in cement manufacture; and motor and steam systems across a number of sectors.
- Congress should consider adopting a carbon tax in the form of an upstream price on fossil fuels for energy production plus industrial non-energy carbon emissions, with the tax corrected for carbon that is captured and stored and carbon in feedstocks permanently embodied in products and compliance with source-specific or cross-sector standards.
- Congress should consider adopting a carbon tax that begins at roughly $20 per metric ton and increases over time based on rising damage from climate change, the revenues from which should be spent for some combination of economic efficiency, income redistribution, and climate policy purposes.
- Congress should alternatively consider an emissions trading scheme (ETS) that operates within strict, multisector emissions limits, with allowances exchanged cross-sector with the potential to expand to other jurisdictions through linked programs, all within a fixed, declining cap that affords minimal or no offsets.
- EPA should adopt regulations under §111(b) and (d) of the CAA for industrial source categories that emit a large share of carbon emissions

and industrial source categories for which technological solutions are readily identified and cost effective.

- EPA should adopt regulations under §115 of the CAA to fix an aggregate limit for industrial carbon emissions that declines to meet deep decarbonization objectives and allows for a variety of compliance options, including emissions trading.
- Congress and the administration should pursue subsidy of deep decarbonization of the industrial sector through a mix of federal research, development, and demonstration (RD&D), tax exemption, and equipment standards (cross-sector); energy audits and voluntary agreements (sector-specific); and information-based programs (sector- and economywide).
- Congress should approve appropriations for an innovation fund that would establish criteria for access to resources (e.g., co-benefits such as cost savings or environmental management systems innovation), to supplement emissions trading encouraged by new EPA rulemaking under CAA §111 and/or §115, and to assist states as they draft state implementation plan (SIP) revisions to comply with rulemaking under the CAA.
- In addition to production emissions and energy use, Congress should require that firms publicly report emissions data by material.
- DOE should modify its Superior Energy Performance initiative to include carbon emissions target setting, material efficiency standards, and reuse and material substitution optimization requirements.
- DOE could inventory material flows; subsidize effective recycling, industrial linkage, and co-processing technologies; and facilitate industrial symbiosis agreements among firms and state and local governments that pursue resource synergies.
- EPA should design emissions trading programs for industrial carbon emissions within or across industry subsectors to achieve significant environmental justice co-benefits.

Part IV

Energy Efficiency, Conservation, and Fuel Switching in Transportation

Chapter 13: Transforming Transportation Demand

by Trip Pollard

Transportation is the leading source of carbon pollution in the United States, and transportation demand is a key determinant of emissions levels. Although the DDPP reports provide valuable analysis of a number of alternatives to slash GHG emissions, they do not investigate transportation demand in any depth. Opportunities to transform transportation are plentiful and could dramatically reduce GHG pollution and check the spread of roads, parking lots, and other aspects of our transportation system that can destroy carbon sinks. Steps should be taken at the federal, state, regional, and local levels to remove subsidies for driving; send better price signals to help internalize the costs of driving; remove barriers to low- and zero-carbon transportation alternatives and provide meaningful rail, transit, bicycling, and walking options; and promote more compact, mixed-use development patterns that can shorten or eliminate trips. These steps often complement each other and are most effective if implemented together. The pressing question is whether the enormous potential to decarbonize transportation will be realized in time to help avoid the worst impacts of climate change. Rapid technological innovation, demographic changes, public support for cleaner transportation choices, and the multiple co-benefits these changes can bring—including health, economic, fiscal, national security, and equity co-benefits—can all help overcome barriers to decarbonizing transportation.

Key Recommendations:

- States and metropolitan planning organizations (MPOs) should add GHG assessment to their transportation planning laws and policies and reorient transportation planning to advance decarbonization.
- Congress and state governments should adopt measures to send better price signals regarding the cost of driving, including increased motor fuel taxes.
- Localities should eliminate free on-street parking, raise parking rates (and consider demand-based parking prices that change to maintain

a certain percentage of vacant spaces), and amend zoning regulations to trim the amount of free parking developers are required to provide.

- The private sector should promote teleworking and telecommuting, and employ flexible and compressed work schedules to reduce peak travel and overall driving.
- Transportation network companies (TNCs) should expand and increase services that work in concert with low- or zero-emission transportation alternatives, including public transit, bicycling, walking, and the use of zero-emission motor vehicles.
- Federal and state governments should devote a larger share of transportation funding to providing meaningful alternatives to driving, and increase funding for projects that better connect various modes in order to expand transportation choices.
- Localities should alter or eliminate sprawl-inducing zoning provisions, such as minimum lot and house sizes, and revamp zoning and building code requirements to promote more compact, mixed-use development.
- State governments and localities should pursue reforms that better link transportation and land use, including targeting transportation funding and planning resources to encourage transit-oriented development (TOD).

Chapter 14: Light-Duty Vehicles

by Amy L. Stein and Joshua P. Fershée

To reduce the United States' GHG emissions by at least 80% from 1990 levels by 2050 will require multiple legal pathways for changing its transportation fuel sources. The DDPP reports characterize the transformation required of the transportation system as part of the third pillar of fundamental changes required in the U.S. energy system: "fuel switching of end uses to electricity and other low-carbon supplies." Relying upon the 2015 DDPP analysis, the chapter addresses that challenge as applied to light-duty vehicles (LDVs) such as cars and sport utility vehicles. Specifically, the DDPP authors anticipate two changes required for our LDV fleet by 2050: (1) increased fuel economy standards in excess of 100 miles per gallon; and (2) deployment of approximately 300 million alternative fuel vehicles, which for purposes of the chapter consists of electric vehicles (EVs), hybrids (electric and gas), and hydrogen vehicles. The goal is to shift 80%-95% of the miles driven from gasoline to lower carbon energy sources like electricity and hydrogen. The chapter identifies key legal pathways to advance these two goals, focusing on actions to both facilitate the growth of alternative fuel vehicles and to limit the production and use of gas- and diesel-fueled vehicles.

Key Recommendations:

- Governmental and private entities should continue to expand financial and other support infrastructure for expanded use of EVs.
- Governmental and private entities should establish programs, incentives, and regulations to facilitate residential, multiunit dwellings, and public-space charging infrastructure.
- Governmental and private entities should assist in R&D toward the goal of reducing battery costs.
- Governmental and private entities should continue to educate dealers, EV employees, and potential consumers about EVs.
- Federal and state legislators should proactively address safety standards, regulations, and liability regimes for autonomous vehicles.

- Governmental and private entities should continue to use their purchasing power to increase demand for EVs.
- Governmental and private entities should consider prioritizing support for expanding the faster growing EV market rather than trying to promote a lagging hydrogen fuel cell vehicle (HFCV) market.
- Utilities should incorporate the demand from EVs in their load forecasts and integrated resource plans and look to EVs, incentive structures to encourage off-peak charging, and the feasibility of EVs serving as grid batteries to ease the flat and declining demand curve projections for electricity.
- The federal government should continue to tighten fuel economy standards.
- State legislatures should use pay-as-you-drive, vehicle miles traveled (VMT) options, or a one-time fee charged to EV owners at the time of registration, to help ensure that alternative vehicles contribute their share to road construction and maintenance.

Chapter 15: Heavy-Duty Vehicles and Freight

by Andrea Hudson Campbell, Avi B. Zevin, and Keturah A. Brown

To achieve an 80% reduction of U.S. GHG emissions by 2050, the DDPP reports state that total CO_2 emissions from the entire transportation sector would have to be cut between 75% and 100% from a 2014 baseline. The chapter discusses the role of heavy-duty vehicles (HDVs) and rail in achieving that goal. Freight transportation results in significant GHG emissions. Decarbonizing this sector will require substantial changes to the two primary means of moving freight within the United States: trucking and rail. In particular, emission standards that facilitate fuel efficiency improvements and conversion to zero- or near-zero-emission technologies such as electric drivetrain technology, hydrogen, and synthetic gas will likely be necessary to achieve 80% reduction in GHG emissions by mid-century. Moreover, shifting from more fuel-intensive but more flexible transportation modes such as trucking, to more efficient but less flexible modes such as rail can play an important role. In addition to environmental regulation, the significant infrastructure requirements of freight transportation will necessitate federal, state, and local financial investments; changes to regulatory models to encourage more and more-optimal private-sector infrastructure investment; and streamlining of permitting and other barriers. To the extent that new or improved infrastructure is required to expand the rail network or provide fueling or charging infrastructure for advanced technology vehicles, decarbonizing the transportation sector could result in significant job creation in the United States.

Key Recommendations:

- EPA, with NHTSA, should consider establishing a post-2027 HDV and engine GHG/fuel economy regulatory program.
- EPA could construe its authority to regulate motor vehicle fuels under the CAA broadly enough to permit the creation of incentives for the construction of the necessary infrastructure to support battery-electric and fuel cell HDVs.

- EPA and DOE should partner to encourage charging and hydrogen refueling infrastructure development.
- Congress could amend EPCA/EISA to provide NHTSA with greater ability to consider effects on human health and the environment when setting standards, rather than requiring the agency to focus only on feasible vehicle fuel efficiency improvements.
- EPA should expand its program to hasten the replacement of less efficient HDVs, including grants and subsidies for individuals and fleet owners.
- Congress should create corporate tax credits to provide incentives for fleet owners to transition to more advanced technology vehicles used to transport or deliver freight.
- The private sector should invest in next-generation HDVs and necessary infrastructure to reduce fleet GHG emissions.
- Federal, state, and local governments should expand investments in rail infrastructure to reduce choke points.
- Federal, state, and local governments should increase investment in freight transportation infrastructure.
- State and local laws, regulations, and ordinances should be amended, as necessary, to streamline siting, permitting, and construction of fueling infrastructure for EVs and HFCVs.

Chapter 16: Aviation

by Aoife O'Leary

Aviation is the most carbon-intensive form of travel and is a significant contributor to climate change. International aviation emissions are growing rapidly and are projected to grow 300% by 2050 if no action is taken. A 2016 report has shown that, in order for international aviation to only consume 12% of the carbon budget that would allow the world to stay within a 1.5°C temperature increase by 2050, the absolute maximum of innovation, operational improvements, and biofuels must be deployed. An ambitious policy to reduce aviation emissions is urgently needed. The United States has not enacted any emissions reduction measures for aviation. There are no substantive legal barriers to the United States doing so, but there are significant political challenges, including strong opposition from the aviation industry and differences of views among the agencies that regulate aviation in the United States, especially EPA and the Federal Aviation Administration (FAA). The International Civil Aviation Organization (ICAO) has been discussing the regulation of aviation emissions for two decades. And within the industry itself, there are a number of efficiency goals and some airlines are beginning to test biofuels. However, the sum of all these efforts will be inadequate to reduce aviation emissions by two-thirds by 2050, as is envisaged in the DDPP reports. The chapter sets forth a variety of measures that, when combined, could put the United States on track to reduce aviation emissions by two-thirds by 2050.

Key Recommendations:

- Congress could adopt an economywide carbon trading or tax measure, including aviation.
- Congress could increase taxes on passenger tickets.
- Congress could place an entirely new tax on aviation with solely a climate purpose.
- FAA should reconsider its guidelines on state aviation taxes and redesign them to allow states to adopt appropriate taxes to reduce aviation emissions.

- Congress could carry out a full review of all the taxes and charges placed on the aviation industry with the explicit objective of considering whether they are adequate in light of aviation's climate impact.
- EPA should adopt a CO_2 emissions standard for aircraft that includes a benchmark intensity system with tradable permits.
- The private sector should enable or encourage less flying.
- The U.S. Department of State should issue an interpretation of the air service agreements to state explicitly that the United States interprets "on the basis of reciprocity" to mean that either Party to the international air service agreement can start taxing international aviation fuel at any time.
- The president—perhaps a new president—should align the policy goals of various agencies and departments to work to reduce aviation emissions to the maximum possible extent.
- Congress should repeal the European Union (EU) Emissions Trading System Prohibition Act.
- The United States could consider working with the EU on a joint aviation emissions reduction measure.

Chapter 17: Shipping

by Aoife O'Leary

International shipping is responsible for 3% of global GHG emissions. Ships departing U.S. ports are responsible for 4.8% of international shipping emissions. U.S. domestic shipping (ships travelling from one U.S. port to another U.S. port) is responsible for only 0.08% of U.S. domestic emissions. International shipping emissions are projected to increase between 50% and 250% by 2050. This means that, on a business-as-usual pathway, total international shipping emissions could reach 18% of global GHG emissions by 2050. Yet, the DDPP reports for the United States do not look closely at shipping. The four 2050 scenarios in the reports all show energy demand for domestic shipping reducing by two-fifths but without much detail on how these reductions are achieved. International shipping is not considered in the reports. The specialized United Nations body for international shipping, the International Maritime Organization (IMO), has estimated that design, operational, and alternative fuel measures could reduce international shipping emissions by 75% by 2050 and that innovative technologies could achieve even further reductions. The legal issues that arise when considering the decarbonization of shipping are mainly jurisdictional. There are three types of authority that countries can exercise over ships: flag (regulating ships that fly the country's flag), coastal (regulating the ships that pass through a country's coastal waters), and port (regulating ships that dock in that country's ports). The chapter concludes that the latter, regulating the ships that dock in U.S. ports (referred to as port jurisdiction under international law), is the most appropriate for controlling GHG emissions.

Key Recommendations:

- Congress could impose a tax or credit system on the basis of the ship's journey to the United States, from the United States, or both.
- Congress should require all ships to track and then report all GHGs emitted from the last port of call to the U.S. port of call, require that information to be made public, and support the development of efficiency rankings.

- EPA should reconsider whether GHG emissions from shipping significantly contribute to air pollution that affects public health and welfare, and subsequently adopt appropriate emissions reductions measures.
- The United States could propose and work to develop consensus for such an international fuel tax for shipping within the IMO.
- The federal government should conduct a careful study of the Jones Act's net impact on emissions from shipping. Subsequently, depending on the results, the Act should then be repealed or amended to include emissions reductions measures as indicated in the study.
- States could formulate their own GHG standards for shipping and submit them to EPA for approval or, alternatively, set in-use requirements without EPA approval.
- Ports can differentiate port charges or fees based on GHG emissions of particular ships.
- Companies with high shipping volumes (e.g., Walmart, IKEA, Nike) could impose supply chain requirements, such as only moving their goods on ships that meet a certain efficiency standard, use a low-carbon fuel, or slow steam.
- The United States could ask the Conference of Parties to the United Nations Framework Convention on Climate Change (UNFCCC) to set a global cap on shipping emissions.

Part V

Electricity Decarbonization

Chapter 18: Utility-Scale Renewables

by Michael B. Gerrard

Achieving the DDPP scenarios to decarbonize the U.S. energy system will require a program of building onshore wind, offshore wind, utility-scale solar, and associated transmission that will exceed what has been done before in the United States by several times, every year out to 2050. These facilities, together with rooftop photovoltaics and other distributed generation (DG), are required to replace most fossil fuel generation and to help furnish the added electricity that will be needed as many uses currently employing fossil fuels (especially passenger transportation and space and water heating) are electrified. The chapter discusses the four most important legal processes and obstacles involved in this enormous project: site acquisition and approval; the National Environmental Policy Act (NEPA); state and local approvals; and species protection laws. It also presents recommendations for lowering the obstacles and briefly discusses several corollary actions that are needed.

Key Recommendations:

- The Bureau of Energy Management (BOEM) should continue its designation of wind energy areas, and prepare programmatic environmental impact statement (EIS) to expedite approval of projects in those areas.
- Congress should instruct reviewing agencies that unavoidable visual and aesthetic impacts do not provide a basis for denying wind energy permits.
- States with offshore wind capacity should develop and implement processes to promptly review and act upon applications for offshore wind projects.
- Federal agencies could increase staffing to review applications for new wind and solar capacity.
- The Council on Environmental Quality (CEQ) should amend its NEPA regulations to provide that a mitigated finding of no significant impact (FONSI) is the preferred method for reviewing certain kinds of

renewable projects if specified types of mitigation measures are undertaken and if the particular site does not pose special problems.

- The federal government should vigorously implement the new Fixing America's Surface Transportation Act (FAST) provisions to achieve the expedited review of renewable energy projects.
- States without adequate laws and procedures in place to review and approve large-scale renewable projects should adopt such laws.
- Congress and state legislatures should enact statutes to prohibit state officials and local governments from banning renewable energy facilities and require state officials and local governments to make decisions in facility siting within a reasonable period of time.
- The U.S. Fish and Wildlife Service (FWS) could develop standard methodologies under the Endangered Species Act (ESA) for mitigation of harms from particular kinds of utility-scale projects.

Chapter 19: Distributed Renewable Energy

by K.K. DuVivier

For individuals, the heating and cooling of buildings is the second largest source of U.S. CO_2 emissions after transportation. The chapter suggests pathways to help deploy the two most promising categories of U.S. distributed renewable energy resources to reduce these emissions—photovoltaic solar matched with storage and thermal sources for hot water and for heating and cooling buildings. DG is probably the energy source most impacted by different levels of government and nongovernmental actors. However, DG is also most immediate to consumers, especially with new technologies or rate structures that give them feedback about their own individual generation and consumption patterns. This, along with exciting new leaps in DG technologies, suggests there are opportunities for DG to play an increasing role in significantly decarbonizing U.S. energy.

Key Recommendations:

- Congress should give residential solar installations the same tax credits as they give to commercial or utility installations.
- States should include in their RPS mandates (1) solar energy, specifically from DG sources, (2) energy storage and microgrid capacity, and (3) thermal energy systems that can contribute to decarbonization.
- States should enact statewide building mandates for ZNE buildings and include the self-generation portion of ZNE buildings in the mandates.
- State public utilities commissions (PUCs) should require utilities to expand the options for using grid-connected photovoltaic (PV) systems along with distributed battery storage to provide the benefits of resilience and emergency backup to their services with strategies such as (1) maintaining net metering until an alternative rate that measures the true value of solar generation is established, (2) requiring time-of-use rates, or transactive rates if possible, and (3) allowing non-utilities to sell excess power to neighbors.

- States should help reduce the soft costs of installing DG solar by simplifying and standardizing the permitting processes and installation requirements for rooftop PV, storage, and solar thermal.
- Nongovernmental organizations should set ambitious goals, such as the 100% renewable energy goal, to maintain pressure on governments and corporations to make efforts to promote DG resources.
- State governments should provide incentives for planned communities to install district heating infrastructure in newly built or remodeled mixed-use zones so that residential construction could take advantage of waste heat.
- Congress or state legislatures should enact laws to recognize and protect the right of landowners to install and operate solar technologies on their properties without significant physical or financial restrictions.
- Utilities, local governments, or nongovernmental organizations should educate those involved in their tree planting campaigns about the impacts tree shadows can have on DG solar energy systems and provide guidance about how to pick tree species (e.g., those with lower maturation heights or those with less sun-blocking foliage or branches) and where to place them to minimize their negative impacts.
- State legislatures should facilitate the deployment of solar installations through third-party ownership (TPO) models and community solar ownership legislation, such as virtual net metering, for all customers.

Chapter 20: Transmission, Distribution and Storage: Grid Integration

by Alexandra B. Klass

The chapter discusses the important role of the electric transmission and distribution grid in meeting deep decarbonization goals. The U.S. DDPP reports state that meeting the 2050 target of reducing U.S. GHG emissions 80% below 1990 levels will require almost "fully decarbonizing" U.S. electricity resources and shifting a large share of transportation-related energy needs from petroleum resources to electricity resources. Accomplishing this goal will require a doubling of U.S. electricity generation as well as a significant expansion of the U.S. electric transmission and distribution grid, particularly since onshore renewable energy resources are dispersed widely throughout the country and are often located far from population centers. The reports conclude that the actual monetary cost to build the necessary transmission and distribution infrastructure is modest and will not significantly impact the cost of electricity resources for consumers. But there are significant legal, political, and socioeconomic barriers to building significant amounts of new, interstate transmission infrastructure. These barriers and potential solutions to them are the focus of the chapter.

Key Recommendations:

- Congress could expand DOE's authority under the Energy Policy Act of 2005 (EPAct 2005) to partner with private transmission line companies in areas beyond the Western Area Power Administration (WAPA) and the Southwestern Power Administration (SWPA).
- Congress could leave siting authority for interstate transmission lines with the states but require that states consider regional and national electricity needs, including decarbonization goals, in making siting decisions and allowing a federal remedy in court for failure to comply.
- Congress, DOE, FERC, and states can fund additional research, technology, and development on a range of distribution network and smart grid developments, including energy storage.

- RTOs, FERC, and other federal agencies should work cooperatively with states on distribution-side developments to ensure that grid operations remain stable as more distributed energy is added to the grid.
- State legislatures could amend existing laws to direct their state PUCs to consider regional and national need as well as clean energy goals in determining whether there is a "need" for a transmission line that will impact the state.
- To the extent state law sets out what is a "public use" for purposes of eminent domain authority, state legislatures could amend the law to make clear that public use includes benefits to a multi-state region as well as to the individual state.
- If state legislation is unclear regarding how to define "need" and "public use," state PUCs can interpret those terms expansively to encompass regional need and regional public use as well as clean energy goals within the state or the region.
- State legislatures and state PUCs could make clear that merchant transmission line companies can seek siting permits and exercise eminent domain authority under the same conditions as electric utilities.
- States should adopt new laws or regulatory policies to create additional flexibility for how to classify energy storage projects for purposes of ratepayer recovery, or other means of rewarding energy storage initiatives, to facilitate greater integration of renewable energy into the grid.
- Transmission line companies should hold community meetings early and often, partner with environmental groups, create local construction partners, and provide direct tax benefits to local communities as well as voluntary payments to the communities on a per-mile basis to reduce opposition to transmission lines.

Chapter 21: Nuclear Energy

by David A. Repka and Tyson R. Smith

The DDPP reports project a doubling of demand in the United States for electricity by 2050, even accounting for increased energy efficiency and conservation. In two DDPP scenarios—the High Nuclear and Mixed Scenarios—this demand would be met by significant increases in nuclear, wind, and solar energy by 2050. The DDPP High Nuclear Scenario involves more than 400 gigawatts of nuclear. This is four times current nuclear capacity in the United States. The DDPP Mixed Scenario involves approximately 200 gigawatts of nuclear capacity, or two times current capacity. A sustained national commitment to nuclear energy in the United States would be necessary to meet the DDPP goals—for either the High Nuclear or Mixed Scenario. Advanced nuclear technologies exist or are under development that could support a significant, rapid expansion of nuclear energy capacity. But under current conditions, those technologies are not likely to be deployed at the scale required to meet the assumptions in either DDPP scenario. The chapter therefore highlights various factors that impact nuclear energy and proposes legal, regulatory, and policy changes to reduce barriers and promote increased use of nuclear generation.

Key Recommendations:

- The federal government should develop a comprehensive program—ideally, a permanent legislated solution—that imposes meaningful restraints on carbon emissions from the electricity sector.
- FERC and states should continue and then complete ongoing efforts to fully value the benefits of nuclear power, including consideration of state-level zero-emissions credit programs.
- State legislatures or utility commissions could impose a nuclear portfolio standard that would co-exist alongside existing RPSs or broaden the scope of existing RPSs to incorporate all "clean" energy, including nuclear power.
- Congress should consider PTCs for nuclear generation to prevent early retirements by "topping off" economic returns for nuclear generators.

- The federal government should consider subsidies for nuclear generation comparable to direct subsidies for renewables that improve, if not reverse, the cost comparison relative to renewables.
- Congress should expand the federal loan guarantee program to be far more extensive in scope, more financially aggressive, and less costly for the project developers than the 2005 program.
- Congress could amend the Atomic Energy Act (AEA) to reduce or eliminate the fee recovery for the government review of new designs that could be considered as a public investment in the technology.
- Congress should consider direct public funding or public-private partnerships to develop, license, and deploy small modular reactors (SMRs) and advanced non-light water reactor (LWR) technologies.
- Congress could increase DOE funding (supplementing private venture capital) to support development and testing of new reactor technologies, as well as detailed design engineering and Nuclear Regulatory Commission (NRC) licensing.
- NRC should—consistent with the AEA and NEPA—eliminate contested hearings on NEPA issues (or at least move them forward in the process).
- The federal government should support transmission systems to connect nuclear power sites to population centers.
- Congress should appropriate funds to reactivate and license the Yucca Mountain project for disposal of spent nuclear fuel.
- Congress could authorize private waste storage facilities (e.g., current proposed facilities in Texas and New Mexico) to store nuclear waste.
- Congress could assign the tasks of completing a repository and addressing the need for additional repository capacity to a new "Nuclear Waste Administration" as an alternative to DOE with a clear mission and consistent funding from the existing Nuclear Waste Fund.

Chapter 22: Hydropower

by Charles R. Sensiba, Michael A. Swiger, and Sharon L. White

While the DDPP reports recognize that pumped storage hydropower is crucial to sustaining our transition to a decarbonized grid, they do not fully account for the potential for environmentally responsible expansion of new conventional hydropower in the United States by 2050. They conclude that conventional hydropower is not expected to keep pace with electricity growth due to sustainability and resource constraints. Yet, additional hydropower development above current levels—both conventional and pumped storage—that meets modern environmental requirements must be a component of any proposal to reduce the United States' dependence on carbon over the long term. Realizing the full potential of hydropower and even maintaining the current hydropower fleet will likely depend on overcoming a number of impediments to hydropower in the United States. Such impediments include lengthy and complex regulatory requirements, failure of the organized electricity markets to adequately compensate hydropower generators for the grid benefits they provide, environmental opposition to new hydropower, and interest in dam removal. These challenges can be overcome with targeted legal and policy reforms that would not roll back environmental standards.

Key Recommendations:

- Congress should adopt a national RPS that includes all forms of duly licensed and exempted nonfederal hydropower, or Congress should adopt a carbon tax.
- Congress should require FERC, together with federal and state resource agencies exercising authority in the licensing or relicensing of nonfederal hydropower, to give "equal consideration" to the climate benefits afforded by hydropower.
- Congress should reform the hydropower licensing and permitting program by statutorily designating FERC as the lead agency, for purposes of NEPA review, for all licenses and other authorizations required under federal law.

- To address state-law requirements requiring the state to conduct any required environmental review in conjunction with state action authorized under federal law, Congress should provide for states to participate as a cooperating agency with FERC, while providing opportunity for states to complete additional reviews under state law that are beyond the scope of NEPA.
- To help reduce redundancy in environmental studies and ensure sufficient time to complete all needed studies, Congress should direct FERC and all other resource agencies to develop a single comprehensive study plan at the beginning of the federal approval process, which will inform agency decision-making under all licensing and permitting requirements under federal law.
- To help promote timely participation by the hydropower applicant and participating resource agencies, Congress should empower FERC to establish a centralized schedule for the completion of all licenses and authorizations required for a nonfederal hydropower project.
- To ensure that all participants meet the deadlines set forth in the centralized schedule, Congress should include appropriate enforcement mechanisms.
- RTOs and independent system operators (ISOs) should enact market rules to accommodate the participation of energy storage (including hydro pumped storage) in energy markets, consistent with FERC's final rule.
- RTOs and ISOs should establish new products and reform existing products that would adequately compensate ancillary services such as those provided by hydropower.
- State PUCs should direct their regulated electric utilities to evaluate the need for and benefits of grid-scale storage such as pumped storage hydropower.
- States should consider including pumped storage hydropower as transmission assets entitled to cost-of-service rate recovery in their transmission planning as an alternative to construction of new transmission lines.

Chapter 23: Electricity Charges, Mandates, and Subsidies

by Jim Rossi

While the DDPP reports identify clear emissions targets and energy resource scenarios that can meet them, they do not tell us which policy levers to pull to get there. The chapter focuses on specific policy changes to electric power mandates, subsidies, and retail customer charges that can help to facilitate the transition to deep decarbonization. Existing state and federal policies regarding these tools demonstrate their potential for balancing economic, consumer welfare, and environmental goals as the electric power system adapts to various DDPP scenarios. It will be necessary to significantly scale up and recalibrate electric power mandates, subsidies, and retail customer charges to successfully arrive at any of the DDPP scenarios in the electric power sector. While no one change to these tools will be sufficient on its own to achieve the DDPP's goals, state regulators, Congress, and federal agencies are well positioned to design a package of reforms to ensure that the transition to deep decarbonization does not impair economic efficiency or consumer welfare.

Key Recommendations:

- States should evaluate new power projects based on their systemwide project costs and benefits, and should favor integrated planning approaches that compare the social costs and benefits of various power projects.
- States should adopt incentives that enable customer behavior/investment choices, including decoupling, customer demand response, and deployment of smart metering.
- State regulators could consider more-flexible cost recovery tools that allow utilities to take advantage of the passage of time, including subjecting project approvals to ongoing prudence review to recognize new information about different technologies and project construction costs.
- States legislatures and utility commissions should encourage local governments to take initiative in building clean energy infrastructure, especially to the extent that this allows them to draw on tax-free financing options.

- Congress should consider adoption of a national carbon tax to encourage investment in new low-carbon energy resources, while also aligning carbon pricing with the broader policies related to the pricing of interstate energy markets.
- Congress should adopt future tax credits based on the decarbonization benefits associated with new investments.
- Congress should adopt a national clean energy standard (CES), including energy efficiency and a national clean energy credit program that would coordinate a national market for tradable credits.
- Congress should adopt legislation allowing low-carbon energy supply resources such as residential solar photovoltaic to presumptively qualify for interconnection and qualifying facility benefits under the Public Utility Regulatory Policies Act (PURPA).
- FERC should adopt a regulation that encourages RTOs to adopt a grid system reliability adder reflecting the carbon attributes of different energy resources in setting transmission rates for the sale of energy in interstate wholesale power markets.
- FERC should issue a policy statement finding that interconnections for renewable power facilities presumptively meet the agency's public interest standard, and clarify how its nondiscrimination standard under §§205 and 206 of the Federal Power Act (FPA) (which require the agency to set just, reasonable, and nondiscriminatory rates) will apply to a decarbonized grid.
- FERC should adopt a rule that clarifies PURPA's application to non-dispatchable resources such as solar and wind, and should avoid granting broad waivers to PURPA mandatory buyback and avoided cost obligations based on a lack of utility market power where market failures impede renewable power projects from having access to competitive interstate markets.
- FERC should clarify the continued permissibility of state clean energy incentives and subsidies unless FERC expressly preempts them in a specific context (e.g., via adjudicative order or adoption of a notice-and-comment rule).

Chapter 24: Phasing Out the Use of Fossil Fuels for the Generation of Electricity

by Steven Weissman and Réna Kakon (with appendices by Stephen Herzenberg and Michael B. Gerrard)

In order to achieve a low-carbon world, it is essential to make the use of energy far more efficient and to introduce a very significant amount of renewable or otherwise carbon-free generation. Yet, these steps alone will not decarbonize electricity. Each scenario in the DDPP reports envisions dramatic reductions in the use of fossil fuels to generate electricity. Fossil-fired generation, utilizing coal and natural gas, provides a lion's share of the gigawatt hours serving end-use customers, and shows no sign of abating. History does not support the assumption that cleaner technologies will push out the dirtier ones. What are needed are affirmative actions designed to phase out the use of fossil fuels to generate electricity. Affirmative steps come in various forms. They start with planning—recognizing current patterns of fossil fuel use and charting a different course. Action can include some combination of specific state and federal prohibitions on the use of fossil fuels by all electric service providers; limits on GHG emissions; closure or divestment of government-owned fossil-fueled generators; and the implementation of policies that have a direct or indirect effect on the cost of power from carbon-emitting sources. The chapter expands on the nature of the challenge and describes the range of solutions in greater detail. The chapter has two appendices. The first, written by Stephen Herzenberg, recommends social policies to accelerate a fossil fuel phaseout. The second, written by Michael Gerrard, recommends ways of addressing stranded assets.

Key Recommendations:

- States with explicit climate policies should insist that utility resource plans reflect a reasonable schedule for ramping down the use of fossil-fired generation.

- States without explicit climate policies should rely on their obligation to ensure that utility rates are just and reasonable to require that resource plans reflect stiffer GHG restrictions that may apply in the years ahead.
- Regional planners, which consist of transmission owners and grid operators in a specific geographical area, should consider what it would take to phase out the use of fossil-fired generation and prepare to meet long-term GHG reduction goals.
- States could impose an outright ban on new coal-fired generation and/or a formal limit on new natural gas generation additions.
- States could put a limit on GHG emissions related to power generation.
- FERC can require that wholesale rates include a carbon adder set at a level intended to reflect the social cost of carbon.
- States could require utility planners to include a carbon adder for planning purposes.
- Municipal utilities and electric cooperatives should divest ownership of their coal-fired generating units.
- State governments could pay utilities the remaining "book value" for investor utility-owned plants, and negotiate prices with private plant owners to pay them to close GHG-emitting facilities.
- States could ban or limit coal mining and oil and gas production.
- State governments should require companies to consider the possibility that their fossil fuel-related assets would be stranded before making investment decisions.
- FERC and state public utility regulators should consider the possibility of stranded assets when assessing proposals for fossil fuel infrastructure that will be paid for by ratepayers.

Key Recommendations From Appendix A:

- As the federal government imposes new carbon taxes, it should use some of the revenues to help workers and communities transition out of the carbon economy.
- Congress could adopt "carbon adjustment assistance" for dislocated carbon workers modeled on Trade Adjustment Assistance for workers dislocated by trade, and move toward an overall "active labor market

system" through which society as a whole covers more of the costs to workers and their families of all economic transitions.

- Congress could use grants, technical assistance, and peer learning to induce more companies to reposition themselves from carbon to non-carbon energy markets, retraining and retaining more of their existing workers.
- Congress should enact and fund the RECLAIM Act of 2017 (H.R. 1731) to provide $1 billion dollars over five years to restore abandoned coal mines and use these and other funds to scale up economic diversification efforts in coal country, including through grants distributed by the Appalachian Regional Commission.
- State legislatures and local governments should promote the creation of more clean energy jobs in coal country.
- State legislatures could allow utilities to charge ratepayers for the cost of industrywide hiring halls and for retraining that bridges the gap between workers' old skills and new occupations.
- States and localities should expand climate change planning and modeling to: (1) analyze what it would take to make workers and regions dependent on carbon jobs whole; and (2) develop plans to achieve a level of equity and "shared prosperity" that would unite community members behind a common battle to reduce carbon emissions.
- Wind, solar, or energy efficiency companies should give hiring preference to displaced coal or coal-fired utility workers; state legislatures could require this within future renewable energy portfolio standards or energy efficiency mandates, while also establishing wage standards that improve job quality in renewable and energy efficiency jobs.

Key Recommendations From Appendix B:

- FERC should consider the possibility of stranded assets when assessing proposals for fossil fuel infrastructure that will be paid for by ratepayers, such as natural gas pipelines and electric transmission lines.
- Fossil fuel companies should, in their securities filings and other disclosures, provide detailed discussions of: (1) how their businesses would transition to a carbon pricing or regulatory system that is consistent with a two degree world; and (2) what will happen to their businesses

and physical assets of the world fails to keep temperatures within two degrees above pre-industrial conditions.

- State public utility commissions should consider the possibility of stranded assets when assessing proposals for fossil fuel infrastructure that will be paid for by ratepayers, such as electric transmission lines and (in states where electric utilities are still vertically integrated) generating facilities.

- The Department of the Interior should halt federal leasing of federal lands and waters for fossil fuel extraction.

Part VI

Fuel Decarbonization

Chapter 25: Bioenergy Feedstocks

by Blake Hudson and Uma Outka

Renewable bioenergy offers an alternative to fossil fuels for transportation and electric power, the two highest GHG-emitting sectors in the United States. Bioenergy feedstocks are cultivated crops, agricultural and forest residues, algae, sewage and livestock manures, and other organic materials. Feedstock selection and cultivation begins the bioenergy supply chain, followed by handling, processing and distribution, and, eventually, end use conversion, producing fuels to power motor vehicles and generate electricity. To achieve deep decarbonization across the U.S. economy, reducing carbon emissions at every stage of the bioenergy supply chain is paramount. As the chapter explains, there are at least four primary pathways for legal reform of the bioenergy feedstocks sector: land use prescriptions that preserve and expand carbon sinks and that ensure feedstocks are cultivated consistent with decarbonization objectives; subsidy programs that create value in land's carbon sink potential and shape cultivation techniques consistent with decarbonization objectives; renewable energy mandates that stipulate credit for feedstocks on certification of approved cultivation methods and land use change criteria; and direct regulation of bioenergy end uses conditioned on feedstock cultivation processes. Although nationwide policy approaches would be most effective on the 2050 time horizon, policies along these pathways may be pursued independently at the federal, state, and local levels, and in some instances via private environmental governance mechanisms. Accordingly, the goal of deep decarbonization warrants legal innovation and reform wherever politically feasible.

Key Recommendations:

- Congress could adopt legislation requiring forests cultivated for bioenergy production to meet sustainability criteria related to water pollution, erosion, biodiversity and habitat protection, and reforestation.
- Congress could require the use of forested or vegetative buffer zones to protect watersheds in agricultural areas, reducing nonpoint source

water pollution, while creating small carbon sinks that could be significant when aggregated.

- Congress could condition the receipt of federal subsidy funds in the agricultural sector on the implementation of sustainable bioenergy feedstock practices.
- State legislatures could adjust commercial forest management programs to more directly integrate deep decarbonization objectives, particularly related to regeneration, regulation (or prevention) of conversion of feedstock forests to other, non-forested uses, and regulation of GHG-emitting technology utilized during the feedstock cultivation process.
- States should consider implementing policies aimed at more stringently regulating, preserving, and expanding forest lands.
- States should adopt policies to keep forests from being converted to cropland, keep natural and biodiverse forests from being converted to biofuel forests, increase carbon sink potential of agricultural soils by forestalling conversion to more carbon-intensive uses, and protect watersheds and biodiversity from natural resource conversion related to residential, industrial, and commercial development.
- States should adopt or expand programs aimed at GHG emissions mitigation or sequestration from the forestry or agricultural sectors.
- Congress could modify the 2007 Renewable Fuel Standard (RFS) to phase out credits for grandfathered facilities.
- Congress could adopt a low-carbon fuel standard to emphasize bioenergy with near-zero lifecycle carbon.
- The federal government could require that any bioenergy companies participating in the market demonstrate certification of sustainable operations before receiving federal permits or other approvals.

Chapter 26: Production and Delivery of Low-Carbon Gaseous Fuels

by Romany M. Webb and Melinda E. Taylor

Recent increases in natural gas use in electricity generation and other applications have been widely heralded as a vital step in the transition to a clean energy economy. Natural gas is often described as a "clean" fossil fuel because its combustion emits significantly less mercury and other air toxins than coal or oil. Natural gas combustion also emits fewer GHGs than other fossil fuels. Any savings at the point of combustion may, however, be offset by GHG emissions during natural gas production. Most of those emissions take the form of methane, a highly potent GHG, released through gas leaks, venting, and flaring (where there is incomplete combustion). To reduce emissions, the DDPP technical report recommends replacing natural gas with renewable gases, such as biogas, hydrogen, and synthetic methane. The chapter discusses various government policies that may be used to support the production and use of renewable gases.

Key Recommendations:

- States should consider adopting RPSs for gas, requiring a minimum percentage of total supply to be met with biogas, hydrogen, and/or synthetic methane.
- States should enact legislation designating a single agency with responsibility for issuing all necessary permits for renewable gas production facilities.
- Local zoning boards should amend their rules to specifically address the development of renewable gas production facilities, unless their definitions of industrial or manufacturing uses are already sufficiently broad.
- State agencies should amend their rules to specifically address the permitting of renewable gas production facilities.

- Congress should enact legislation directing DOE or another agency to provide grants for renewable gas production facility development and appropriate funding therefor.
- Congress should enact legislation authorizing the provision of loan guarantees for renewable gas projects by DOE.
- State legislatures should designate a lead agency with responsibility for coordinating the various permitting processes for renewable gas gathering pipelines.
- State PUCs should adopt renewable gas quality standards that do not operate as a barrier to pipeline transportation.
- FERC and state PUCs should require pipeline operators seeking to apply stricter quality standards to renewable gas than natural gas to provide a valid justification for that choice.
- The Pipeline and Hazardous Materials Safety Administration (PHMSA) should adopt more-stringent repair requirements for renewable gas pipelines to minimize pipeline leaks and associated costs.

Chapter 27: Production and Delivery of Bioenergy Fuels

by James M. Van Nostrand

Biomass energy, or bioenergy, is expected to play a prominent part in achieving a deeply decarbonized energy system, according to the analysis in the DDPP reports. While decarbonization will focus largely on the use of electricity where possible—electricity becomes a much larger share of final energy under the decarbonization strategies—there are "high-value end uses" that are less amenable to electrification, such as freight transport and industry. For these nonelectric end uses, biomass is envisioned to become a major fuel source. The reports recommend shifting current biofuels policy from production of corn-based ethanol and gasoline substitutes and redirecting biomass resources toward these high-value end uses. This scaled-up role for bioenergy correspondingly stimulates the pursuit of decarbonization opportunities throughout the biofuels supply chain. The chapter focuses on opportunities for decarbonization in the "middle" elements of the biofuels supply chain—the production of bioenergy, and the transportation logistics before and after the production process. Achieving the necessary level of decarbonization in the production and delivery of biofuels will require a variety of legal strategies, including reformation of the RFS, widespread adoption of low-carbon fuel standards by states and regions, and measures to promote carbon intensity reductions in the production of biofuels, such as increased use of combined heat and power to reduce dependence upon grid electricity (until such time as the electrical grid is substantially decarbonized), and carbon capture and sequestration (CCS) at biorefineries.

Key Recommendations:

- Congress should reform the RFS approach to include a multiplier for per-unit emissions reductions.
- Congress should reform the 2010 RFS to move from an absolute volume of mandated production to a percentage of final demand, which will be necessary as overall gasoline demand declines due to the improvements in the transportation sector.

- The federal government (specifically, DOE and the U.S. Department of Agriculture (USDA)) should redeploy funding for biofuels research to development of fuels that have high-value uses, such as biomass-based diesel.
- Congress and/or state legislatures should adopt measures to stimulate investment in barge and rail transport—such as tax incentives or additional public investment rail and river infrastructure—that could result in displacement of truck transportation for biofuel feedstocks and biofuels.
- Congress and/or state legislatures should provide tax credits or grant funding to stimulate investment in R&D focused on the costs and benefits of pre-transport processing of feedstocks.
- State legislatures should include combined heat and power in their state RPS or EERS.
- Retail utilities should develop "standard offer programs" that would stimulate investment in distributed energy resources—and combined heat and power in particular—for industrial customers, including biorefineries.
- Congress, state legislatures, or local governments should adopt measures that would stimulate investment in biofuels receiving terminals—such as tax incentives or grants for eligible terminal improvements—to facilitate increased use of rail transport for biofuels delivery.
- Congress and/or state legislatures should provide incentives to encourage the construction of pipelines that are dedicated to the delivery of ethanol and biofuels.
- FERC should adopt a policy statement calling for a higher rate of return on the equity investment in pipelines that are dedicated to the delivery of ethanol and biofuels.

Part VII

Carbon Capture and Negative Emissions

Chapter 28: Carbon Capture and Sequestration

by Wendy B. Jacobs and Michael T. Craig

The chapter addresses the use of CCS to achieve significant reductions in emissions of CO_2 to the atmosphere by 2050. Regardless of one's views about the cause, pace, or even existence of climate change, the time is ripe to drive CCS forward. National and state investment in and support of CCS are completely consistent with the Trump Administration's goals to (1) invest in infrastructure projects; (2) continue U.S. reliance on fossil fuels; (3) create jobs; and (4) make America great. CCS can help achieve these goals and more. The chapter provides an overview and explains why, despite much study and decades of use of the technology, its widespread adoption in the United States has not yet occurred. The chapter also describes the potential of CCS for achieving deep decarbonization of the U.S. power sector and explains the key components of CCS. The chapter identifies and recommends several federal and state legal reforms necessary to drive CCS forward.

Key Recommendations:

- States should impose restrictions on CO_2 emissions to drive CCS. For example, states can adopt carbon emissions standards on new sources that require full CCS on new coal-fired units by the early 2020s, and partial and full CCS on new natural gas combined cycle (NGCC) units by the mid-2020s and early 2030s, respectively.
- States should expand their RPS laws to become CESs, mandating not just the purchase of renewable energy, but also energy produced by coal-fired and NGCC plants that are equipped to capture CO_2.
- State governors should issue executive orders to (1) direct agencies to purchase a minimum amount of CCS-produced energy; and (2) significantly raise the minimum total amount of clean energy to be purchased by the state government by 2050, where the grid includes plants that are or can be equipped with CCS.

- States and/or regions could form and fund agencies akin to public utilities to conduct siting analyses, acquire property access rights, and otherwise coordinate and facilitate expansion of the CO_2 pipeline network.
- State PUCs can help stabilize and subsidize prices for CCS-generated electricity by a variety of mechanisms, including approvals of rates to help defray the cost of CCS and power purchase agreements (PPAs).
- Congress should authorize the U.S. Department of the Interior and DOE to own and control several sequestration sites.
- Congress should expand tax credit programs under §§48A and 48B of the Internal Revenue Code by (1) explicitly extending them to NGCC plants that capture CO_2; (2) enlarging the five-year time frame; and (3) appropriating additional funds.
- Congress should expand the existing PTC for renewable generation to include electricity that is produced by plants that use CCS.
- Congress should require emitters and storers of CO_2 to pay a fee to fund a liability program in exchange for certain limits on their potential liability for damages resulting from sequestration.
- Congress should enact legislation to encourage private investment in CCS technology via private activity bonds (PABs).
- The president should issue an Executive Order to: (1) direct agencies to purchase a minimum amount of CCS-produced energy; and (2) significantly raise the minimum total amount of clean energy to be purchased by the federal government by 2050.
- EPA should in the near term tighten the new source performance standards (NSPS) under the CAA for new coal-fired and NGCC units to levels only achievable with CCS or partial CCS.

Chapter 29: Negative Emissions Technologies and Direct Air Capture

by Tracy Hester

Given the U.S. economy's continuing reliance on fossil fuel energy sources and the high levels of anthropogenic GHGs already in the atmosphere, a full deep decarbonization pathway assessment will have to explore the use of negative emissions technologies (NETs), which include the direct air capture (DAC) of ambient CO_2. NETs are technologies that capture or consume more CO_2 than they emit on a cumulative basis, and DAC, loosely defined, is a subset of NETs that use any industrialized chemical or physical methods to remove GHGs from the ambient atmosphere and then store or reuse those gases typically in a way that does not allow them to escape back into the atmosphere. While still nascent, NETs include a wide array of approaches such as biomass energy with CCS, enhanced weathering of minerals, and the direct mechanical capture of ambient CO_2 through filters and chemicals. The chapter focuses on the legal pathways needed to accelerate the development and use of NETs and assure their proper governance.

Key Recommendations:

- The federal government should explicitly endorse and support research, development, and implementation of NETs as appropriate in conjunction with other decarbonization strategies.
- To achieve CO_2 removal at the necessary scale within a relevant time frame, Congress and state legislatures should significantly boost the funding available to support NET research proposals.
- Congress should impose a carbon tax or other pricing mechanism that would expressly allow NET operators to obtain a financial return on the CO_2 they capture from the atmosphere.
- Federal and state government can reduce barriers to NETs from legal requirements, environmental permitting requirements, or environmental impact reviews in a manner that will not expose the public or the environment to unwarranted environmental risks.

- State governments should consider the designation of carbon removal technologies as an accepted method to attain RPS targets.
- Congress and the federal agencies could explore the possibility of offering certain liability protections for NET operators that meet size, operational, and safety requirements.
- EPA and state environmental agencies can adopt: (1) standardized approval and review procedures for NETs that use common procedures or similar physical designs; and (2) general permits for NETs that will likely have either small or predictable and controlled impacts to the environment.
- EPA and state environmental agencies could promote the reuse of captured CO_2 as a feedstock or commercial product by issuing guidance or a regulatory determination that CO_2 captured through NETs would not constitute a pollutant or waste under federal and state environmental statutes if reused.

Chapter 30: Agriculture

by Peter H. Lehner and Nathan A. Rosenberg

The chapter examines the agricultural strategies, practices, and technologies available to increase soil carbon sequestration and reduce GHG emissions. It summarizes on the research documenting the many agricultural practices that have been demonstrated to reduce GHG emissions and increase carbon sequestration in soil, including cover cropping, more varied crop rotations, agroforestry and silvopasture (adding trees into cropping or grazing systems), perennial crops, prescribed rotational grazing, dry manure management, and others It details pathways for amending existing federal and state legal regimes and enacting new ones, and recommends improving public agricultural research, development, and extension efforts; reforming federal subsidy and conservation programs; and revising trade policy, tax policy, regulatory strategies, financing for carbon farming, grazing practices on government land, and GHG pricing. It also describes how the private and philanthropic sectors can stimulate carbon farming; strategies for reducing emissions that stem from farm inputs and that result from food processing, distribution, consumption, and waste; and the potential to encourage consumption of climate-friendly foods through national dietary guidelines, procurement at all levels of government, and private-sector initiatives such as certification schemes and healthier menu options. The chapter notes that many of the practices recommended to reduce agriculture's contribution to climate change also will make farms and ranches more resilient to extreme weather and often increase soil health, productivity, and profitability. There can thus be a confluence of interests supporting incentives for broader adoption of these practices.

Key Recommendations

- Congress should prioritize funding for conservation programs that offer the greatest climate benefits, while reducing or eliminating funding that benefits environmentally harmful operations.
- Congress should adopt a farm safety net focused on payments for ecosystem services (i.e., payment for improved stewardship and environmental benefits such as climate stabilization or water quality or quantity) in place of much or all of the current programs.

- Congress should significantly expand funding to support climate-friendly practices at all research and extension entities within USDA, including the Agricultural Research Service, the National Institute of Food and Agriculture, the Sustainable Agriculture Research and Education program, Climate Hubs, and the Cooperative State Research and Extension Service, in order to achieve carbon neutrality while maintaining crop and livestock productivity.
- Congress should at a minimum double the extension system's budget to $900 million, designating the additional funds for climate change-related education, programming, and services.
- The Risk Management Agency (RMA) should ensure that its crop insurance policies do not interfere with cover cropping or other proven decarbonizing practices or conversely encourage less beneficial practices.
- The Federal Crop Insurance Corporation (FCIC) should require publicly funded crop insurance policies to treat GHG-intensive practices as risk enhancing and reduce or eliminate their premium subsidies accordingly.
- Congress should expand funding for the Conservation Reserve Program (CRP), while also reforming CRP to provide sustained climate benefits by offering farmers 30-year agreements or permanent easements, targeting lands with the most significant climate-change mitigation and adaptation potential.
- Congress should redirect Environmental Quality Incentives Program (EQIP) funds, to the extent possible, to support farms and ranches working to significantly reduce emissions or sequester carbon.
- The Natural Resources Conservation Service (NRCS) should revise the Conservation Stewardship Program (CSP) to prioritize low-carbon practices and to create a funding pool for farmers transitioning to, or practicing, carbon farming.
- Congress should expand funding for the CSP to prioritize climate-beneficial activities like cover crops and resource-conserving crop rotations and ensure that they receive a higher, supplemental payment.
- Congress should authorize EPA, states, localities, and private citizens to enforce conservation compliance requirements with a citizen-suit-type provision in addition to the current USDA enforcement.

- Congress should expand the required practices for conservation compliance to include those that protect soil carbon and water.
- EPA should replace its "aggregate compliance" approach to ensuring that biofuel feedstock is not produced on newly converted cropland and replace it with an individualized compliance requirement, and not allow the conversion of CRP land.
- Congress should integrate climate concerns into agricultural trade policy, mandating that USDA and other government agencies focus on developing markets for climate-friendly products and discontinue support for carbon-intensive commodities.
- State legislatures should consider adopting a fertilizer fee that could both encourage more judicious use of fertilizer and help fund training on how to ensure no yield losses with less fertilizer and other climate-friendly agricultural practices.
- State governments should consider requiring farm owners to comply with basic climate-friendly practices, such as installing buffer strips next to streams, in order to receive tax benefits for agricultural activities or easements.
- EPA should strengthen its nationwide national pollutant discharge elimination system (NPDES) regulations in ways that would reduce GHG emissions as well as water pollution.
- USDA should ensure that government financial incentive and regulatory programs do not support large-scale operations without also requiring them to curb their most environmentally damaging practices.
- Congress should require the Farm Service Agency (FSA) and the Farm Credit System lending institutions to offer programs providing favorable credit to farmers and ranchers using climate-friendly practices recognized by NRCS and to require minimum climate-friendly practices relating to all loans.
- The Bureau of Land Management (BLM) should enforce lease provisions that require ranchers to uphold conservation values, and add new ones designed to reduce the climate impacts of grazing systems.
- BLM should undertake a process to update the grazing intensity limit in leases to reflect current conditions, including range quality, climate, and animal size.

- Congress should create lending institutions, or existing ones could create specialty divisions, aimed at financing farms using climate-friendly practices.
- Agricultural land trusts should incorporate climate change mitigation into easement purposes, ensuring that easement conditions encourage climate-friendly practices and that farmers' efforts to mitigate climate change do not conflict with their easements.
- States should adopt legislation banning food waste in landfills, using Vermont's Universal Recycling Law as a model.
- Local governments, through their own purchasing, advertising, or public support, could also encourage a wider range of whole or minimally processed plant-based options, and other climate-friendly options, at restaurants.

Chapter 31: Forestry

by Federico Cheever with
Robert B. McKinstry, Jr., and Robert L. Fischman

Forests and forest management have significant roles to play in addressing climate change in the United States. U.S. forests currently sequester nearly 40 gigatons (Gt) of carbon and are growing at a rate that offsets about 700 million tons (0.7 Gt) of CO_2 emissions per year, roughly 10% of U.S. total emissions. Forest management in the coming decades could increase forest carbon capture by another 100 million tons per year. However, forests and forest sequestration cannot substitute for emissions reduction in the long term, since forests will eventually reach steady state, where CO_2 uptake and release are roughly in balance. Achieving an additional 100 million tons of sequestration per year will present significant challenges, requiring the addition of 2.7 million newly forested acres per year for the next several decades, as the amount of additional land suitable for reforestation declines. Moreover, many existing forests will be stressed by the climate changes that are now inevitable, and those same changes will reduce the areas that can support forests. Failure to manage forests with climate change in mind will result in significant additional carbon releases as trees are assaulted by wildfire, insect infestation, and disease increased by a changing climate. This makes the deep decarbonization necessary to stabilize climate all the more difficult.

Because forest ownership and authority in the United States are distributed among the federal government, state governments, local governments, and private owners, a variety of legal tools must be employed to realize the potential for carbon sequestration and limit the potential damage of climate change. Federal, state, and local governments all have parts to play. National and state laws and regulations should require carbon sequestration tracking and provide credits for sequestration in sustainably managed forests in emissions trading programs. Federal and state programs should include additional incentives for use of biomass generated from "low-use" wood produced through sustainably managed forests in programs to replace fossil fuels for local heating and cooling and to co-fire biomass in electricity generating stations with the CCS capacity. Incentives include local land use regulation and conservation easements to protect existing forests and to encourage reforestation that will sequester carbon, private certification of carbon sequestering forests, and conservation tax incentives to enhance carbon capture on private land.

Key Recommendations:

- Congress could amend the "organic legislation" that sets out comprehensive management charters for each federal public land system by mandating consideration and implementation of climate change mitigation, adaptation, and resilience in plans for the management of federal lands, including requirements for maximization of carbon storage in trees and soils, the use of low-use and excess wood for production of energy, and use of public lands for geologic sequestration.
- Federal land management agencies should implement the same types of climate change mitigation and adaptation and resilience programs through the broad, discretionary authority provided by the existing organic acts.
- Federal, state, and local governments should expand publicly owned forests by acquiring and reforesting private lands, focusing on lands rendered economically unproductive by the effects of climate change.
- Congress should impose a meaningful carbon tax (or auction) and create a CO_2 trading regime in which sequestration in forests, soils, and forest products is specifically recognized.
- The president should use executive authority to create and expand national monuments and manage federal lands to promote afforestation of permafrost areas, as climate change supports the expansion of northern forests.
- EPA should use existing authority under the CAA to create an auction cap-and-trade program giving credit for sequestration of carbon in forests, forest products, and soils and recognition that use of low-use wood from sustainably managed forests will not add CO_2 to the atmosphere.
- State legislatures should amend state forestry laws to recognize the importance of considering carbon capture, geologic sequestration, and climate change adaptation in management decisions regarding state forests, specifically authorizing those actions, while state foresters should use existing authority to the same end.

- State legislatures should enact, or state governors should use existing authority to implement, a carbon tax or GHG auction-cap-and-trade program that recognizes private forest CCS through afforestation, avoided deforestation, and improved forest management; incorporates carbon in long-lived forest products as an emission offset; exempts emissions from sustainably produced biomass; and imposes a cost on those who deforest their land through conversion.
- The American Forest and Paper Association and the Forest Stewardship Council should include in their sustainable forestry certification programs standards maximizing the potential for forestry CCS.
- USDA should develop and promote a national climate-friendly wood product certification system analogous to its system for certifying organic produce.

Part VIII

Non-Carbon Dioxide Climate Pollutants

Chapter 32: Black Carbon

by Melissa Powers

Black carbon (or soot) is a potent climate forcer that may rank second only to CO_2 in warming the planet. Reducing black carbon emissions could avoid as much as .5°C (or nearly 1° Fahrenheit) of warming. In the United States, the major sources of black carbon emissions are diesel combustion from the transportation sector, diesel combustion from stationary sources, coal combustion, and biomass combustion. The chapter discusses key strategies and obstacles to reducing black carbon emissions, with a particular focus on reducing diesel fuel use. The chapter explains how several CAA programs that regulate emissions of fine particulate matter (PM), including the mobile source standards program, several stationary source programs, national ambient air quality standards, and SIPS, could help reduce or eliminate black carbon emissions. The chapter also examines programs that state and local governments could use independent of the CAA to reduce black carbon emissions. Finally, the chapter identifies obstacles to successful regulation, proposes strategies to overcome obstacles, identifies areas of uncertainty, and briefly identifies measures discussed in other chapters in the book that would complement or accelerate the black carbon reduction strategies identified here.

Key Recommendations

- EPA should prioritize regulations that accelerate fleet turnover and otherwise take older and dirtier engines and vehicles off the road.
- As clean fuels from renewable energy become available, EPA should require their use in diesel engines.
- EPA should mandate that all diesel sources use diesel particulate filters (DPFs) to reduce both PM and black carbon emissions.
- If EPA changes its approach of deferring to California when reviewing waiver requests, California should vigorously protect the California waiver by suing EPA.
- California should continue to use its ability to enact and strengthen state mobile source standards.

- Other states should adopt California emission standards and work closely with California to identify priorities for future standards, identify the local benefits of adopting the California standards, and expose the risks of delaying action.
- Local governments should enact in-use restrictions that prohibit idling of all vehicles, but particularly heavy-duty diesel vehicles.
- States should enact indirect source rules to limit the extent to which stationary sources attract and encourage mobile source emissions.
- States should develop and implement transportation plans that are designed to achieve zero-emission transportation systems.
- EPA should require stationary sources to install the most effective PM filters and other emissions controls.
- States should develop comprehensive woodstove replacement programs, accompanied by funding necessary to enable low-income access to modern technologies, to accelerate turnover.
- Federal and state land management agencies should develop prescribed burn protocols and land management strategies to minimize the net warming caused by emissions of PM and CO_2.

Chapter 33: Methane

by Steven Ferrey with Romany M. Webb

Short-lived climate chemical pollutants, such as methane, exert a much more powerful climate impact than CO_2 in the near term. The IPCC estimates that, in the first 20 years after it is released, methane traps 84 times more heat in the earth's atmosphere than CO_2 (on a per ton basis), while other researchers suggest it could be even more of a near-term warming agent. Given this, and with methane the second most dominant climate-warming chemical, reducing emissions is vital to avoid dangerous climate change. The DDPP technical report for the United States indicates that, to limit warming to 2°C or less, GHG emissions must be reduced by 80% below 1990 levels by 2050. The United States is not currently on track to meet that goal with respect to methane. Any emissions reduction strategy must target the three largest anthropogenic sources of methane (i.e., fossil fuel production and transportation, agriculture, and waste management), which together account for 96% of national emissions. In each sector, emissions can be reduced by employing available technologies to capture methane, and utilizing it as an energy source. While this benefits emitters, reducing their energy costs and/or generating additional revenues (e.g., from the sale of captured methane), many facilities are yet to deploy capture systems. The chapter addresses the technological pathways to reduce methane emissions in the fossil fuel, agriculture, and waste management sectors, and identify barriers to their adoption. The chapter outlines regulatory reforms needed to overcome those barriers and otherwise support emissions reductions.

Key Recommendations

- EPA could reinstate its NSPS for new oil and gas facilities, if they are rescinded during the Trump Administration.
- In the absence of federal action to control methane emissions from oil and gas production, states can adopt their own emissions reduction measures.
- State environmental agencies can consider adopting regulations to cost effectively control venting, flaring, and leaks from well sites.

- State PUCs could change existing cost recovery frameworks where they discourage repair by, for example, imposing the risk of increased leakage entirely on customers.
- States could establish their own funding programs for anaerobic digester projects.
- Federal and state governments should adopt programs to fund gas management systems at both municipal and private landfills, and prioritize awards to landfills investing in landfill gas (LFG)-to-energy systems.
- EPA's 2016 CAA regulations for methane emissions from municipal solid waste landfills could be retained and made even more stringent.
- EPA could revise its Resource Conservation and Recovery Act (RCRA) regulations to prevent landfill operators from venting methane to the atmosphere.
- States could restructure or amend their air pollution and other laws to impose the same or stricter requirements on the venting and flaring of biogas from wastewater treatment facilities, as apply to its use in electricity generation and other applications.

Chapter 34: Fluorinated Gases

by Nathan Borgford-Parnell, Stephen Oliver Andersen, and Durwood Zaelke

The chapter covers fluorinated GHGs, namely hydrofluorocarbons (HFCs). The DDPP reports seek to reduce HFC and hydrochlorofluorocarbon (HCFC) emissions in the United States by 96 million metric tons (MMT) CO_2 equivalent (CO_2eq) by 2050. HFCs replaced chlorofluorocarbons (CFCs) and HCFCs that have been phased out under the Montreal Protocol on Substances That Deplete the Ozone Layer because they were depleting the stratospheric ozone layer. Due largely to their use as substitutes for CFCs and HCFCs, HFCs are the fastest growing GHGs in the United States, growing from 0.3 MMT CO_2eq in 1990 to 149.4 MMT CO_2eq in 2010. EPA, many states, and businesses have already begun acting to speed the phasedown of HFCs in the United States. There are a number of legal pathways at the federal, state, and local levels that would further reduce emissions of HFCs and speed markets to a safe transition to environmentally friendly alternatives. Additional climate benefits can be realized by simultaneously improving the energy efficiency of equipment during the transition away from high-global warming potential (GWP) refrigerants.

Key Recommendations:

- The federal government should quickly ratify the Kigali Amendment either through an Executive Order based on existing authority to regulate HFCs under Title VI of the CAA or formal advice and consent by the U.S. Senate.
- State legislatures should adopt legislation and state governors should adopt executive orders mandating that state and local government agencies identify measures to reduce HFC emissions.
- State and local governments should update and amend their green purchasing program requirements to eliminate purchases of HFC-containing equipment where other low-GWP and more energy-efficient alternatives are available on the market.

- Federal, state, and local governments should use life-cycle climate performance (LCCP) accounting in their energy-efficiency programs and regulations.
- Congress could amend EPCA to apply a full LCCP accounting of regulated appliances.
- States could work collaboratively to issue collective standards for LCCP on consumer appliances for which no federal standard has been issued.
- The U.S. Green Building Council could amend the Leadership in Energy and Environmental Design (LEED) certification to make the use of low-GWP refrigerants and high energy-efficiency prerequisites for qualifying for credit.
- Utilities should include low-GWP refrigerants in their energy-efficiency incentive programs.
- Standards and code-making bodies should continue research and testing for all sectors to ensure the rapid and safe deployment of new low-GWP cooling and refrigeration technologies and equipment.

Chapter 35: Nitrous Oxide

by Jessica Wentz and David Kanter

Nitrous oxide emissions are the third largest driver of climate change and the single greatest threat to the stratospheric ozone layer. They accounted for approximately 5% of total U.S. GHG emissions in 2015 (measured in CO_2eq). Key sources of nitrous oxide include agricultural soil and manure management, stationary and mobile combustion, and industrial processes such as adipic and nitric acid production. These sources account for 95% of U.S. nitrous oxide emissions. EPA estimates that U.S. nitrous oxide emissions will increase approximately 18.5% over 2015 levels by 2030, and these increases will come primarily from the agricultural sector. The DDPP reports conclude that nitrous oxide emissions should be reduced by at least 70 million tons CO_2eq in 2050 relative to a business-as-usual baseline to achieve an overall net GHG emission reduction of 80% below 1990 levels by 2050. The chapter explains how existing legal pathways or new legal mechanisms could be used to attain and even exceed this reduction target.

Key Recommendations

- EPA and state environmental authorities should seek to regulate nitrous oxide emissions from agriculture and livestock through management standards, rather than direct emission caps, due to the complexities of monitoring, verifying, and enforcing compliance with emissions caps for these sectors.
- EPA should use its authority under CAA §§115 or 615 to issue nationwide regulations respecting the control of nitrous oxide emissions from agricultural soil management and livestock.
- EPA should use its authority under CAA §§111, 115, or 615 to establish emission caps or performance standards for stationary sources of nitrous oxide emissions, particularly power plants and nitric acid facilities.
- EPA should continue to use its authority under CAA §202 to regulate mobile sources of nitrous oxide emissions, and should introduce more stringent nitrous oxide emission caps for new motor vehicle fleets.
- When designing and implementing cap-and-trade programs, EPA, state regulators, and regional authorities should incentivize nitrous

oxide emission reductions from agricultural and livestock sources by providing offset credit for such reductions.

- Federal and state agricultural agencies should invest in technical support programs aimed at educating farmers about "win-win" measures—specifically, management strategies that improve nitrogen use efficiency, reduce fertilizer requirements, and reduce nitrous oxide emissions.

Key Recommendations Organized by Actor

This index organizes all of the recommendations set forth in this volume by actor (e.g., local governments), enabling readers to see in one place all of the key recommendations for any particular actor, regardless of the chapter in which they originated. Each recommendation notes the chapter in which it appears. When the larger volume, *Legal Pathways to Deep Decarbonization in the United States,* is published, an updated version of this index that provides specific page numbers to the larger volume will be available for download at https://www.eli.org/DeepDecarbKeyRecommendations. Note that the index below does not contain the full collection of recommendations provided in the larger volume, also organized by actor.

U.S. Government, Generally

- The federal government should assess all near-term decisions against long-term goals and viable pathways to achieve them, balancing replacing retiring fossil fuel based infrastructure with available low-carbon technologies, in order to help minimize carbon lock-in and stranded assets. (Ch. 1)
- The federal government should engage in integrated planning based on the efficient and transparent sharing of information between stakeholders, many of whom have not historically coordinated their efforts. (Ch. 1)
- The federal government should address generational-scale lifestyle changes in two ways: playing offense, particularly when policymakers confront forks in the road where some lifestyle shifts could facilitate deep decarbonization, and playing defense by heading off lifestyle shifts that could undermine deep decarbonization. (Ch. 3)
- The federal government should adopt and implement policy measures to reduce demand for energy services, not just to reduce the energy needed to supply those services. (Ch. 3)
- The federal government should adopt and implement specific strategies that target increased uptake of more energy-efficient home equipment

technologies, including green leases and improved life-cycle cost information for retailers and householders. (Ch. 3)

- The federal government should consider using specific strategies to increase adoption of household-level renewable energy systems and purchases of products with low life-cycle emissions, such as informal marketing through neighborhoods and social networks and targeted marketing to environmentally minded consumers. (Ch. 3)
- The federal government should further use, test, and evaluate specific strategies for motor vehicle efficiency, including improved energy labeling and vehicle fleet buyers' use of supply chain pressure. (Ch. 3)
- The federal government should further use, test, and evaluate specific strategies to increase the uptake of energy-efficient buildings, including energy audits of existing homes and energy rating systems for new homes. (Ch. 3)
- The federal government should further use, test, and evaluate specific strategies to reduce carbon emissions from the use of existing and new home equipment and buildings, including provision of monthly feedback and implementation of information campaigns. (Ch. 3)
- The federal government should further use, test, and evaluate strategies for reducing carbon emissions from the use of existing and new motor vehicles and other forms of transportation, including provision of immediate fuel use feedback devices and development of eco-driving education programs. (Ch. 3)
- The federal government should consider a rejuvenated and focused green patenting program for decarbonization technologies. (Ch. 4)
- The federal government should consider government-funded competitions and prizes to incentivize low-carbon technologies in addition to or instead of traditional research grants or contracts. (Ch. 4)
- The federal government should coordinate with state and local governments, as well as corporations and businesses, to carefully plan technological change inducement programs. (Ch. 4)
- The federal government should provide direct funding of R&D for carbon reduction technologies. (Ch. 4)

- The federal government should provide expedited regulatory approval pathways for some clean technologies, but take care to minimize the risk that such "short cuts" ignore unintended effects or preclude public input. (Ch. 4)
- The federal government should provide subsidies for clean energy technologies and remove current subsidies for fossil fuels and other non-sustainable activities and products. (Ch. 4)
- Assuming that the production tax credit will not continue past its phaseout date, the federal government should assess the need for new incentives, similar to a production tax credit, which would permit continued growth for renewable technologies. (Ch. 5)
- The federal government should support financing of carbon reducing technologies through the issuance of green bonds. (Ch. 5)
- The federal government should work together with state governments and the private sector to study and understand the effects that incentives like the production tax credit have on the growth of renewable technologies. (Ch. 5)
- The federal government should work with state governments and the private sector to continually assess and adjust incentives like the investment tax credit in order to promote the advancement of new technologies. (Ch. 5)
- Wherever the federal government has jurisdiction over an energy project participant, it should use its authority to require reporting of carbon performance information on an ongoing basis. (Ch. 6)
- The U.S. government should consider feed-in tariffs as long as they comply with applicable trade rules. (Ch. 8)
- If federal the government designs a decarbonization law that contains local content requirements, it should meet the national treatment requirements under Article III of the General Agreement on Tariffs and Trade. (Ch. 8)
- The federal government should devote a larger share of transportation funding to providing meaningful alternatives to driving, and increase funding for projects that better connect various modes in order to expand transportation choices. (Ch. 13)

- The federal government can call upon current alternative vehicle owners to educate potential consumers about alternative fuel vehicles (AFVs). (Ch. 14)
- The federal government can work with state governments to standardize the chargers that are being deployed in AFVs and in charging stations by requiring a single standard or by encouraging nongovernmental organizations to work toward a dominant standard. (Ch. 14)
- The federal government should assist in research and development (R&D) toward the goal of reducing battery costs. (Ch. 14)
- The federal government should consider prioritizing support for expanding the faster growing market (i.e., electric vehicles (EVs)), rather than trying to promote a lagging hydrogen fuel cell vehicle market. (Ch. 14)
- The federal government should continue the recent trend of tightening fuel economy and greenhouse gas emissions standards for light-duty motor vehicles. (Ch. 14)
- The federal government should create programs to train EV employees. (Ch. 14)
- The federal government should proactively address safety standards, regulations, and liability regimes for autonomous vehicles. (Ch. 14)
- The United States could consider working with the European Union on a joint aviation emissions reduction measure. (Ch. 16)
- The federal government should conduct a careful study of the "Jones Act's" net impact on emissions from shipping. Subsequently, depending on the results, the Act should then be repealed or amended to include emissions reductions measures as indicated in the study. (Ch. 17)
- The United States could ask the Conference of Parties to the United Nations Framework Convention on Climate Change to set a global cap on shipping emissions. (Ch. 17)
- The United States could propose and work to develop consensus for such an international fuel tax for shipping within the International Maritime Organization. (Ch. 17)
- The federal government should vigorously implement the new Fixing America's Surface Transportation Act provisions to achieve the expedited review of renewable energy projects. (Ch. 18)

- The federal government should consider subsidies for nuclear generation comparable to direct subsidies for renewables that improve, if not reverse, the cost comparison relative to renewables. (Ch. 21)
- The federal government should develop a comprehensive program—ideally, a permanent legislated solution—that imposes meaningful restraints on carbon emissions from the electricity sector. (Ch. 21)
- The federal government should support transmission systems to connect nuclear power sites to population centers. (Ch. 21)
- As the federal government imposes new carbon taxes, it should use some of the revenues to help workers and communities transition out of the carbon economy. (Ch. 24 App. A)
- The federal government could require that any bioenergy companies participating in the market demonstrate certification of sustainable operations before receiving federal permits or other approvals. (Ch. 25)
- The federal government can reduce barriers to negative emissions technologies from legal requirements, environmental permitting requirements, or environmental impact reviews in a manner that will not expose the public or the environment to unwarranted environmental risks. (Ch. 29)
- The federal government should explicitly endorse and support research, development, and implementation of negative emissions technologies as appropriate in conjunction with other decarbonization strategies. (Ch. 29)
- The federal government should quickly ratify the Kigali Amendment either through an Executive Order based on existing authority to regulate hydrofluorocarbons under Title VI of the Clean Air Act or formal advice and consent by the U.S. Senate. (Ch. 34)
- The federal government should use life-cycle climate performance accounting in their energy efficiency programs and regulations. (Ch. 34)

Congress

- Congress should consider adopting a carbon tax that begins at $25 per metric ton, increases over time based on rising damage from climate change, and the revenues from which are spent for some combination of economic efficiency, income redistribution, and climate policy purposes. (Ch. 2)

- Congress should adopt an appropriate carbon tax as the centerpiece of a comprehensive and coordinated strategy to meet deep decarbonization pathways, and set the level high enough to incentivize the deployment of clean technologies. (Ch. 4)
- Congress should induce higher levels of research and development (R&D) in the private sector through an R&D tax credit for carbon reduction technologies. (Ch. 4)
- Congress should put in place a strategy for inducing technological innovation for decarbonization, or authorize an existing or new entity within the federal government to perform this function. (Ch. 4)
- Congress should consider adopting loan programs similar to the Advanced Technology Vehicles Manufacturing Loan Program that are aimed at the development of more efficient renewable energy production. (Ch. 5)
- Congress should expand the pool of investors that can claim the tax incentives for investments in renewable energy generation by offering tax incentives in the form of cash grants. (Ch. 5)
- Congress should act to allow subsidy funds to be combined with private finance to create low-income housing rehabilitation programs that require energy-efficiency standards be met in the rehabilitation process. (Ch. 6)
- Congress should establish an agency that can purchase loans and issue asset-backed securities for residential and small business energy efficiency and renewable energy loans and provide credit support for clean energy lending, including through sustainable finance organizations. (Ch. 6)
- Congress should impose a uniform carbon price on all energy suppliers to give decarbonization investments at the grid edge a competitive advantage without distorting markets. (Ch. 6)
- Congress could pass legislation that establishes extended producer responsibility for a wide range of products. (Ch. 7)

- Congress could pass legislation that establishes life-cycle assessment and disclosure requirements for a wide range of materials and products. (Ch. 7)
- Congress could pass legislation that establishes minimum state recycling rates and food scrap diversion rates. (Ch. 7)
- Congress could pass legislation that establishes procurement requirements for the federal government consistent with circular economy and deep decarbonization goals. (Ch. 7)
- Congress could pass legislation that funds research and development into alternative biomaterials that can substitute for plastics. (Ch. 7)
- Congress could pass legislation that sets forth minimum recycled content requirements for a wide range of materials and products. (Ch. 7)
- Congress should continue to use subsidies (preferably without local content requirements) in the form of tax credits, accelerated depreciation, or cash grants, in combination with other incentives, to help create a market for renewable energy that would eventually drive down some of the production costs. (Ch. 8)
- Congress should structure decarbonization labeling schemes so as not to discriminate against foreign imports. (Ch. 8)
- If Congress adopts decarbonization laws, they must comply with international trade rules. (Ch. 8)
- If Congress decides to adopt a local content requirement for decarbonization, it could limit the requirement to government procurement, particularly if it is linked to decarbonization policies or protection of public health. (Ch. 8)
- Congress should amend the EPCA to explicitly authorize DOE to adopt energy efficiency standards with multiple efficiency metrics. (Ch. 9)
- Congress should amend the EPCA to give DOE discretion to establish shorter compliance lead times for energy efficiency standards when needed and appropriate. (Ch. 9)
- Congress should amend the state preemption provision of the EPCA to provide states with greater autonomy in setting energy efficiency standards. (Ch. 9)

- Congress should approve budgets for DOE's Appliance Standards and Building Codes Program at a level sufficient to support the staff and resources needed to complete required energy efficiency rulemakings on time. (Ch. 9)
- Congress should broaden DOE's authority under the EPCA to cover new products. (Ch. 9)
- Congress should develop an integrated suite of energy efficiency policies that combine, coordinate, and synthesize a full suite of complementary energy efficiency policies, including mandatory minimum energy efficiency standards, voluntary labeling and incentive programs that further increase produce energy efficiency levels over time, tax incentives, and other complementary energy efficiency policies that are part of a larger set of decarbonization policies. (Ch. 9)
- Congress should enact legislation to create an ambitious federal energy-efficiency resource standard, which would be a national energy-efficiency goal for electric and natural gas utilities. (Ch. 9)
- Congress should expand funding and ensure full implementation of key federal low-income energy programs, including the Low Income Home Energy Assistance Program, and the Weatherization Assistance Program. (Ch. 9)
- Congress should consider adopting mandatory retrofit laws for energy conservation and decarbonization in existing commercial and residential buildings. (Ch. 11)
- Congress should consider enacting laws requiring that building owners who presently use fossil fuel for space and water heating must retrofit their buildings by electrification. (Ch. 11)
- Congress should consider legislation requiring that all federal buildings, regardless of age, have no fossil fuel-generated energy consumption on or before 2050. (Ch. 11)
- Congress should consider requiring an energy audit upon the sale or rental of existing homes and commercial properties. (Ch. 11)
- Congress could inventory and amend its scattered minimum efficiency performance standards statutes to provide DOE with explicit authority to set material efficiency goals, remove materially inefficient manufac-

turing incentives, and adjust social cost of carbon figures to reflect new data. (Ch. 12)

- Congress could pass comprehensive product standard legislation modeled after the European Union's Ecodesign Directive. (Ch. 12)
- Congress should adopt a federal subsidy for mid-range energy efficiency and fuel switching in the industrial sector through a sectoral crediting mechanism. (Ch. 12)
- Congress should alternatively consider an emissions trading scheme that operates within strict, multisector emissions limits, with allowances exchanged cross-sector with the potential to expand to other jurisdictions through linked programs, all within a fixed, declining cap that affords minimal or no offsets. (Ch. 12)
- Congress should approve appropriations for an innovation fund that would establish criteria for access to resources (e.g., co-benefits such as cost savings or environmental management systems innovation), to supplement emissions trading encouraged by new EPA rulemaking under Clean Air Act (CAA) §111 and/or §115, and to assist states as they draft state implementation plan revisions to comply with rulemaking under the CAA. (Ch. 12)
- Congress should consider adopting a carbon tax in the form of an upstream price on fossil fuels for energy production plus industrial non-energy carbon emissions (e.g., clinker production), with the tax corrected for carbon that is captured and stored and carbon in feedstocks permanently embodied in products and compliance with source-specific or cross-sector standards. (Ch. 12)
- Congress should consider adopting a carbon tax that begins at roughly $20 per metric ton and increases over time based on rising damage from climate change, the revenues from which should be spent for some combination of economic efficiency, income redistribution, and climate policy purposes. (Ch. 12)
- Congress should employ a mix of policies to drive material efficiency across the life cycle. (Ch. 12)
- Congress should focus on key processes that take place within energy-intensive industries, such as fractional distillation in refineries; steam cracking in petrochemical plants; pulp making, drying, and finish-

ing in paper production; preservation, process heating, and machine-driven end uses in food processing; upstream production approaches in the iron and steel sector; conversion of bauxite to alumina and its electrolysis; clinker production in cement manufacture; and motor and steam systems across a number of sectors. (Ch. 12)

- Congress should promote available and near-term best available technologies (BATs) to shore up the process efficiency of major industrial sectors and lower direct carbon emissions. (Ch. 12)
- Congress should pursue a diverse portfolio of legal tools, including carbon pricing; ad hoc or comprehensive regulatory regimes where a carbon price is set through market mechanisms that respond to emissions standards; subsidies that target emissions at the high and low ends of the carbon emissions abatement cost curve; a sectoral crediting mechanism for beyond-BAT emissions reductions; improved federal motor and boiler minimum efficiency performance standards to address cross-sector leakage in national emissions trading; harmonized state equipment efficiency standards that are not addressed by federal mandate; and a regulatory floor to encourage material efficiency. (Ch. 12)
- Congress should pursue material efficiency strategies such as light-weighting, reduced yield loss, diverted scrap, reuse, increased product life-span, and greater product use intensity. (Ch. 12)
- Congress should pursue policies that promote efficient end use in the industrial sector, energy supply strategies such as electricity supply decarbonization, fuel switching, material efficiency, and carbon management. (Ch. 12)
- Congress should pursue subsidy of deep decarbonization of the industrial sector through a mix of federal research, development, and demonstration, tax exemption, and equipment standards (cross-sector); energy audits and voluntary agreements (sector-specific); and information-based programs (sector- and economywide). (Ch. 12)
- Congress should supplement carbon pricing with subsidies for research, development, and demonstration (RD&D) for measures toward the high end of the carbon emissions abatement cost curve. (Ch. 12)
- Congress should support material efficiency with certification, labeling, and standard-setting as well as preferential purchasing and targeted RD&D support (e.g., R&D integration through DOE's Energy

Materials Network consortia led by one or more national laboratories). (Ch. 12)

- In addition to production emissions and energy use, Congress should require that firms publicly report emissions data by material. (Ch. 12)
- Congress should adopt measures to send better price signals regarding the cost of driving, including increased motor fuel taxes. (Ch. 13)
- Congress should continue to expand financial and other support infrastructure for expanded use of electric vehicles. (Ch. 14)
- Congress could adopt an economywide carbon trading or tax measure, including aviation. (Ch. 16)
- Congress could carry out a full review of all the taxes and charges placed on the aviation industry with the explicit objective of considering whether they are adequate in light of aviation's climate impact. (Ch. 16)
- Congress could increase taxes on passenger tickets. (Ch. 16)
- Congress could place an entirely new tax on aviation with solely a climate purpose. (Ch. 16)
- Congress should repeal the European Union Emissions Trading System Prohibition Act. (Ch. 16)
- Congress could impose a tax or credit system on the basis of the ship's journey to the United States (or from the United States or both ways). (Ch. 17)
- Congress should consider imposing special requirements upon shipping in the Arctic. (Ch. 17)
- Congress should require all ships to track and then report all greenhouse gases emitted from the last port of call to the U.S. port of call, require that information to be made public, and support the development of efficiency rankings. (Ch. 17)
- Congress should enact a statute to prohibit state and local governments from banning renewable energy facilities and require state and local governments to make decisions in facility siting within a reasonable period of time. (Ch. 18)

- Congress should instruct reviewing agencies that unavoidable visual and aesthetic impacts do not provide a basis for denying wind energy permits. (Ch. 18)
- Congress could enact a law to recognize and protect the right of landowners to install and operate solar technologies on their properties without significant restrictions. (Ch. 19)
- Congress should give residential solar installations the same tax credits as commercial or utility installations. (Ch. 19)
- Congress can fund additional research, technology, and development on a range of distribution network and smart grid developments, including energy storage. (Ch.20)
- Congress could expand DOE's authority under the Energy Policy Act of 2005 to partner with private transmission line companies in areas beyond the Western Area Power Administration and the Southwestern Power Administration. (Ch. 20)
- Congress could leave siting authority for interstate transmission lines with the states but require that states consider regional and national electricity needs, including decarbonization goals, in making siting decisions and allowing a federal remedy in court for failure to comply. (Ch. 20)
- Congress could amend the Atomic Energy Act to reduce or eliminate the fee recovery for the government review of new designs could be considered as a public investment in the technology. (Ch. 21)
- Congress could assign the tasks of completing a repository and addressing the need for additional repository capacity to a new "Nuclear Waste Administration" as an alternative to DOE with a clear mission and consistent funding from the existing Nuclear Waste Fund. (Ch. 21)
- Congress could authorize private waste storage facilities (e.g., current proposed facilities in Texas and New Mexico) to store nuclear waste. (Ch. 21)
- Congress could increase DOE funding (supplementing private venture capital) to support development and testing of new reactor technologies, as well as detailed design engineering and Nuclear Regulatory Commission licensing. (Ch. 21)

- Congress should appropriate funds for reactivating and licensing the Yucca Mountain project for disposal of spent nuclear fuel. (Ch. 21)
- Congress should consider direct public funding or public-private partnerships to develop, license, and deploy small modular reactors and advanced non-light water reactor technologies. (Ch. 21)
- Congress should consider production tax credits for nuclear generation to prevent early retirements by "topping off" economic returns for nuclear generators. (Ch. 21)
- Congress should expand the federal loan guarantee program to be far more extensive in scope, more financially aggressive, and less costly for the project developers than the 2005 program. (Ch. 21)
- Congress should adopt a national renewable portfolio standard that includes all forms of duly licensed and exempted nonfederal hydropower, or Congress should adopt a carbon tax. (Ch. 22)
- Congress should reform the hydropower licensing and permitting program by statutorily designating the Federal Energy Regulatory Commission (FERC) as the lead agency, for purposes of National Environmental Policy Act (NEPA) review, for all licenses and other authorizations required under federal law. (Ch. 22)
- Congress should require FERC, together with federal and state resource agencies exercising authority in the licensing or relicensing of nonfederal hydropower, to give "equal consideration" to the climate benefits afforded by hydropower. (Ch. 22)
- To address state-law requirements requiring the state to conduct any required environmental review in conjunction with state action authorized under federal law, Congress should provide for states to participate as a cooperating agency with FERC, while providing opportunity for states to complete additional reviews under state law that are beyond the scope of NEPA. (Ch. 22)
- To ensure that all participants meet the deadlines set forth in the centralized schedule, Congress should include appropriate enforcement mechanisms. (Ch. 22)
- To help promote timely participation by the hydropower applicant and participating resource agencies, Congress should empower FERC to

establish a centralized schedule for the completion of all licenses and authorizations required for a nonfederal hydropower project. (Ch. 22)

- To help reduce redundancy in environmental studies and ensure sufficient time to complete all needed studies, Congress should direct FERC and all other resource agencies to develop a single comprehensive study plan at the beginning of the federal approval process, which will inform agency decisionmaking under all licensing and permitting requirements under federal law. (Ch. 22)
- Congress should adopt a national clean energy standard, including energy efficiency and a national clean energy credit program that would coordinate a national market for tradable credits. (Ch. 23)
- Congress should adopt future tax credits based on the decarbonization benefits associated with new investments. (Ch. 23)
- Congress should adopt legislation allowing low-carbon energy supply resources such as residential solar photovoltaic to presumptively qualify for interconnection and qualifying facility benefits under the Public Utility Regulatory Policies Act. (Ch. 23)
- Congress should consider adoption of a national carbon tax to encourage investment in new low-carbon energy resources, while also aligning carbon pricing with the broader policies related to the pricing of interstate energy markets. (Ch. 23)
- Congress could adopt "carbon adjustment assistance" for dislocated carbon workers modeled on Trade Adjustment Assistance for workers dislocated by trade, and move toward an overall "active labor market system" through which society as a whole covers more of the costs to workers and their families of all economic transitions. (Ch. 24 App. A)
- Congress could use grants, technical assistance, and peer learning to induce more companies to reposition themselves from carbon to noncarbon energy markets, retraining and retaining more of their existing workers. (Ch. 24 App. A)
- Congress should enact and fund the RECLAIM Act of 2017 (H.R. 1731) to provide $1 billion dollars over five years to restore abandoned coal mines and use these and other funds to scale up economic diversification efforts in coal country, including through grants distributed by the Appalachian Regional Commission. (Ch. 24 App. A)

- Congress could adopt a low carbon fuel standard to emphasize bioenergy with near zero lifecycle carbon. (Ch. 25)
- Congress could adopt legislation requiring forests cultivated for bioenergy production to meet sustainability criteria related to water pollution, erosion, biodiversity and habitat protection, and reforestation. (Ch. 25)
- Congress could condition the receipt of federal subsidy funds in the agricultural sector on the implementation of sustainable bioenergy feedstock practices. (Ch. 25)
- Congress could modify the renewable fuel standard to phase out credits for grandfathered facilities. (Ch. 25)
- Congress could require the use of forested or vegetative buffer zones to protect watersheds in agricultural areas, reducing nonpoint source water pollution, while creating small carbon sinks that could be significant when aggregated. (Ch. 25)
- Congress should enact legislation authorizing the provision of loan guarantees for renewable gas projects by DOE. (Ch. 26)
- Congress should enact legislation directing DOE or another agency to provide grants for renewable gas production facility development and appropriate funding therefor. (Ch. 26)
- Congress could provide tax credits or grant funding to stimulate investment in research and development focused on the costs and benefits of pre-transport processing of feedstocks. (Ch. 27)
- Congress should adopt measures that would stimulate investment in barge and rail transport—such as tax incentives or additional public investment in intermodal facilities—to allow increased use of rail transport for feedstock production. (Ch. 27)
- Congress should adopt measures that would stimulate investment in biofuels receiving terminals—such as tax incentives or grants for eligible terminal improvements—to facilitate increased use of rail transport for biofuels delivery. (Ch. 27)
- Congress should provide incentives to encourage the construction of pipelines that are dedicated to the delivery of ethanol and biofuels. (Ch. 27)

- Congress should reform the 2010 Renewable Fuel Standard to move from an absolute volume of mandated production to a percentage of final demand, which will be necessary as overall gasoline demand declines due to the improvements in the transportation sector. (Ch. 27)
- Congress should reform the Renewable Fuel Standard approach to include a multiplier for per-unit emissions reductions. (Ch. 27)
- Congress can authorize the U.S. Department of Interior and the U.S. Department of Energy (DOE) to own and control several sequestration sites. (Ch. 28)
- Congress can expand tax credit programs under §§48A and 48B of the Internal Revenue Code by (1) explicitly extending them to natural gas combined cycle plants that capture carbon dioxide; (2) enlarging the five-year time frame; and (3) appropriating additional funds. (Ch. 28)
- Congress could enact legislation to encourage private investment in carbon capture and sequestration (CCS) technology via private activity bonds. (Ch. 28)
- Congress could expand the existing production tax credit for renewable generation to include electricity that is produced by plants that use CCS. (Ch. 28)
- Congress could require emitters and storers of carbon dioxide to pay a fee to fund a liability program in exchange for certain limits on their potential liability for damages resulting from sequestration. (Ch. 28)
- Congress could explore the possibility of offering certain liability protections for negative emissions technology operators that meet size, operational, and safety requirements. (Ch. 29)
- Congress should impose a carbon tax or other pricing mechanism that would expressly allow negative emissions technology (NET) operators to obtain a financial return on the CO2 they capture from the atmosphere. (Ch. 29)
- To achieve carbon dioxide removal at the necessary scale within a relevant time frame, Congress should significantly boost the funding available to support NET research proposals. (Ch. 29)
- Congress should adopt a farm safety net focused on payments for ecosystem services (i.e., payment for improved stewardship and envi-

ronmental benefits such as climate stabilization or water quality or quantity) in place of much or all of the current programs. (Ch. 30)

- Congress should at a minimum double the extension system's budget to $900 million, designating the additional funds for climate change-related education, programming, and services. (Ch. 30)
- Congress should authorize the U.S. Environmental Protection Agency, states, localities, and private citizens to enforce conservation compliance requirements with a citizen-suit-type provision in addition to current U.S. Department of Agriculture enforcement. (Ch. 30)
- Congress should create lending institutions, or existing ones could create specialty divisions, aimed at financing farms using climate-friendly practices. (Ch. 30)
- Congress should expand funding for the Conservation Reserve Program (CRP), while also reforming CRP to provide sustained climate benefits by offering farmers 30-year agreements or permanent easements, targeting lands with the most significant climate-change mitigation and adaptation potential. (Ch. 30)
- Congress should expand funding for the Conservation Stewardship Program to prioritize climate-beneficial activities like cover crops and resource-conserving crop rotations and ensure that they receive a higher, supplemental payment. (Ch. 30)
- Congress should expand the required practices for conservation compliance to include those that protect soil carbon and water. (Ch. 30)
- Congress should integrate climate concerns into agricultural trade policy, mandating that the U.S. Department of Agriculture (USDA) and other government agencies focus on developing markets for climate-friendly products and discontinue support for carbon-intensive commodities. (Ch. 30)
- Congress should prioritize funding for conservation programs that offer the greatest climate benefits, while reducing or eliminating funding that benefits environmentally harmful operations. (Ch. 30)
- Congress should redirect Environmental Quality Incentives Program funds, to the extent possible, to support farms and ranches working to significantly reduce emissions or sequester carbon. (Ch. 30)

- Congress should require the Farm Service Agency and the Farm Credit System lending institutions to offer programs providing favorable credit to farmers and ranchers using climate-friendly practices recognized by Natural Resources Conservation Service and to require minimum climate-friendly practices relating to all loans. (Ch. 30)
- Congress should significantly expand funding to support climate-friendly practices at all research and extension entities within USDA (including Agricultural Research Service, National Institute of Food and Agriculture, the Sustainable Agriculture Research and Education program, Climate Hubs, and the Cooperative State Research and Extension Service) in order to achieve carbon neutrality while maintaining crop and livestock productivity. (Ch. 30)
- Congress could amend the "organic legislation" that sets out comprehensive management charters for each federal public land system by authorizing geologic sequestration on public lands. (Ch. 31)
- Congress could amend the "organic legislation" that sets out comprehensive management charters for each federal public land system by mandating consideration and implementation of climate change mitigation and adaptation in plans for the management of federal lands, including requirements for maximization of carbon storage in trees and soils, as well as the use of low-use and excess wood for production of energy. (Ch. 31)
- Congress could amend the "organic legislation" that sets out comprehensive management charters for each federal public land system by requiring consideration of resilience actions. (Ch. 31)
- Congress could expand the national forests by acquiring and reforesting private lands, focusing on lands rendered economically unproductive by the effects of climate change. (Ch. 31)
- Congress should impose a meaningful carbon tax (or auction) and create a carbon dioxide trading regime in which sequestration in forests, soils, and forest products is specifically recognized. (Ch. 31)
- Congress could amend the Energy Policy and Conservation Act (EPCA) to apply a full life-cycle climate performance accounting of regulated appliances. (Ch. 34)

Executive Branch

- The executive branch should develop an integrated suite of energy efficiency policies that combine, co-ordinate, and synthesize a full suite of complementary energy efficiency policies, including mandatory minimum energy efficiency standards, voluntary labeling and incentive programs that further increase produce energy efficiency levels over time, tax incentives, and other complementary energy efficiency policies that are part of a larger set of decarbonization policies. (Ch. 9)
- The administration should focus on key processes that take place within energy-intensive industries, such as fractional distillation in refineries; steam cracking in petrochemical plants; pulp making, drying, and finishing in paper production; preservation, process heating, and machine-driven end uses in food processing; upstream production approaches in the iron and steel sector; conversion of bauxite to alumina and its electrolysis; clinker production in cement manufacture; and motor and steam systems across a number of sectors. (Ch. 12)
- The administration should promote available and near-term best available technology (BAT) to shore up the process efficiency of major industrial sectors and lower direct carbon emissions. (Ch. 12)
- The administration should pursue a diverse portfolio of legal tools, including carbon pricing; ad hoc or comprehensive regulatory regimes where a carbon price is set through market mechanisms that respond to emissions standards; subsidies that target emissions at the high and low ends of the carbon emissions abatement cost curve; a sectoral crediting mechanism for beyond-BAT emissions reductions; improved federal motor and boiler minimum efficiency performance standards to address cross-sector leakage in national emissions trading; harmonized state equipment efficiency standards that are not addressed by federal mandate; and a regulatory floor to encourage material efficiency. (Ch. 12)
- The administration should pursue material efficiency strategies such as lightweighting, reduced yield loss, diverted scrap, reuse, increased product life-span, and greater product use intensity. (Ch. 12)
- The administration should pursue policies that promote efficient end use in the industrial sector, energy supply strategies such as electricity

supply decarbonization, fuel switching, material efficiency, and carbon management. (Ch. 12)

- The administration should pursue subsidy of deep decarbonization of the industrial sector through a mix of federal research, development, and demonstration, tax exemption, and equipment standards (cross-sector); energy audits and voluntary agreements (sector-specific); and information-based programs (sector- and economywide). (Ch. 12)
- The president should align the policy goals of various agencies and departments to work to reduce aviation emissions to the maximum possible extent. (Ch. 16)
- The president could issue an Executive Order to (1) direct agencies to purchase a minimum amount of carbon capture and sequestration-produced energy; and (2) significantly raise the minimum total amount of clean energy to be purchased by the federal government by 2050. (Ch. 28)
- The president should use executive authority to create and expand national monuments and manage federal lands to promote afforestation of permafrost areas, as climate change supports the expansion of northern forests. (Ch. 31)

Federal Agencies & Departments, Generally

- If federal agencies, such as the U.S. Environmental Protection Agency, National Highway Traffic Safety Administration, and U.S. Department of Energy that adopt and enforce regulatory standards responsible for reducing greenhouse gas emissions seek to achieve the deep decarbonization targets they should adopt, review, and revise such standards as appropriate to ensure they are consistent and synergistic with deep decarbonization pathways. (Ch. 4)
- Federal agencies should consider adopting loan programs similar to the Advanced Technology Vehicles Manufacturing Loan Program that are aimed at the development of more efficient renewable energy production. (Ch. 5)
- Federal agencies should fully implement the requirement in Energy Independence and Security Act that federal buildings reduce fossil fuel use measured against a 2003 benchmark by 100% by 2030, and meet

the goal that all new commercial buildings achieve zero net energy by 2030. (Ch. 10)

- Federal agencies could increase staffing to review applications for new wind and solar capacity. (Ch. 18)
- Federal agencies should work cooperatively with states on distribution-side developments to ensure that grid operations remain stable as more distributed energy is added to the grid. (Ch. 20)
- Federal agencies could explore the possibility of offering certain liability protections for negative emissions technology operators that meet size, operational, and safety requirements. (Ch. 29)
- Federal land management agencies could implement climate change mitigation and adaptation programs through the broad, discretionary authority provided by the existing organic acts. (Ch. 31)
- Federal land management agencies should develop prescribed burn protocols and land management strategies to minimize the net warming caused by emissions of fine particulate matter and carbon dioxide. (Ch. 32)
- Federal agricultural agencies should invest in technical support programs aimed at educating farmers about "win-win" measures—specifically, management strategies that improve nitrogen use efficiency, reduce fertilizer requirements, and reduce nitrous oxide emissions. (Ch. 35)

U.S. Department of Energy (DOE)

- DOE should continue and enhance coordination with the DOE energy efficiency standards program and the ENERGY STAR. As part of this coordination, ENERGY STAR product ratings should be updated frequently so that voluntary ENERGY STAR ratings can increase market penetration for efficient products, helping to give rise to stronger mandatory DOE energy efficiency standards over time. (Ch. 9)
- DOE should develop an integrated suite of energy efficiency policies that combine, co-ordinate, and synthesize a full suite of complementary energy efficiency policies, including mandatory minimum energy efficiency standards, voluntary labeling and incentive programs that further increase produce energy efficiency levels over time, tax incen-

tives, and other complementary energy efficiency policies that are part of a larger set of decarbonization policies. (Ch. 9)

- DOE should continue setting leading-edge energy-efficiency standards for heating, cooling, lighting, and other energy-consuming equipment used in new buildings. (Ch. 10)
- DOE could adopt motor and boiler minimum efficiency performance standards to address cross-sector leakage under a Clean Air Act §115-enacted emissions trading scheme. (Ch. 12)
- DOE could inventory material flows; subsidize effective recycling, industrial linkage, and co-processing technologies; and facilitate industrial symbiosis agreements among firms and state and local governments that pursue resource synergies. (Ch. 12)
- DOE should modify its Superior Energy Performance initiative to include carbon emissions target setting, material efficiency standards, and reuse and material substitution optimization requirements. (Ch. 12)
- DOE can fund additional research, technology, and development on a range of distribution network and smart grid developments, including energy storage. (Ch. 20)
- DOE should redeploy funding for biofuels research to development of fuels that have high-value uses, such as biomass-based diesel. (Ch. 27)

U.S. Environmental Protection Agency (EPA)

- EPA should consider developing a tiered system for ENERGY STAR ratings that distinguishes the most efficient products. (Ch. 9)
- EPA could adopt regulations under §115 of the Clean Air Act (CAA) to fix an aggregate limit for industrial carbon emissions that declines to meet deep decarbonization objectives and allows for a variety of compliance options, including emissions trading. (Ch. 12)
- EPA should adopt regulations under §111(b) and (d) of the CAA for industrial source categories that emit a large share of carbon emissions and industrial source categories for which technological solutions are readily identified and cost effective. (Ch. 12)

- EPA should design emissions trading programs for industrial carbon emissions within or across industry subsectors to achieve significant environmental justice co-benefits. (Ch. 12)
- EPA should adopt a carbon dioxide emissions standard for aircraft that includes a benchmark intensity system with tradable permits. (Ch. 16)
- EPA should reconsider whether greenhouse gas emissions from shipping significantly contribute to air pollution that affects public health and welfare, and subsequently adopt appropriate emissions reductions measures. (Ch. 17)
- EPA should in the near term tighten the new source performance standards under the CAA for new coal-fired and natural gas combined cycle units to levels only achievable with carbon capture and sequestration (CCS) or partial CCS. (Ch. 28)
- EPA can adopt: (1) standardized approval and review procedures for negative emissions technologies (NETs) that use common procedures or similar physical designs; and (2) general permits for NETs that will likely have either small or predictable and controlled impacts to the environment. (Ch. 29)
- EPA could promote the reuse of captured carbon dioxide as a feedstock or commercial product by issuing guidance or a regulatory determination that carbon dioxide captured through negative emission technologies would not constitute a pollutant under the CWA or CAA or a discarded hazardous waste or substance under RCRA or CERCLA if reused. (Ch. 29)
- EPA should replace its "aggregate compliance" approach to ensuring that biofuel feedstock is not produced on newly converted cropland and replace it with an individualized compliance requirement, and not allow the conversion of Conservation Reserve Program land. (Ch. 30)
- EPA should strengthen its nationwide national pollutant discharge elimination system regulations in ways that would reduce greenhouse gas emissions as well as water pollution. (Ch. 30)
- EPA should use existing authority under the CAA to create an auction cap-and-trade program giving credit for sequestration of carbon in forests, forest products and soils and recognition that use of low use

wood from sustainably managed forests will not add carbon dioxide to the atmosphere. (Ch. 31)

- As clean fuels from renewable energy become available, EPA should require their use in diesel engines. (Ch. 32)
- EPA should mandate that all diesel sources use diesel particulate filters to reduce both particulate matter and black carbon emissions. (Ch. 32)
- EPA should prioritize regulations that accelerate fleet turnover and otherwise take older and dirtier engines and vehicles off the road. (Ch. 32)
- EPA should require stationary sources to install the most effective particulate matter filters and other emissions controls. (Ch. 32)
- EPA could reinstate its new source performance standards for new oil and gas facilities, if they are rescinded during the Trump Administration. (Ch. 33)
- EPA should continue to use its authority under CAA §202 to regulate mobile sources of nitrous oxide emissions, and should introduce more stringent nitrous oxide emission caps for new motor vehicle fleets. (Ch. 35)
- EPA should seek to regulate nitrous oxide emissions from agriculture and livestock through management standards, rather than direct emission caps, due to the complexities of monitoring, verifying, and enforcing compliance with emissions caps for these sectors. (Ch. 35)
- EPA should use its authority under CAA §§115, 615, or 111 to establish emission caps or performance standards for stationary sources of nitrous oxide emissions, particularly power plants and nitric acid facilities. (Ch. 35)
- EPA should use its authority under CAA §§115 or 615 to issue nationwide regulations respecting the control of nitrous oxide emissions from agricultural soil management and livestock. (Ch. 35)
- When designing and implementing cap-and-trade programs, EPA should incentivize nitrous oxide emission reductions from agricultural and livestock sources by providing offset credit for such reductions. (Ch. 35)

Federal Energy Regulatory Commission (FERC)

- FERC could require the establishment of regional transmission organizations (RTOs) throughout the country. (Ch. 6)
- FERC should continue to work toward non-discriminatory "market participation models" that take account of the specific characteristics and capabilities of grid-edge resources. (Ch. 6)
- FERC can fund additional research, technology, and development on a range of distribution network and smart grid developments, including energy storage. (Ch. 20)
- FERC should work cooperatively with states on distribution-side developments to ensure that grid operations remain stable as more distributed energy is added to the grid. (Ch. 20)
- FERC should continue and then complete ongoing efforts to fully value the benefits of nuclear power. (Ch. 21)
- FERC should adopt a regulation that encourages RTOs to adopt a grid system reliability adder reflecting the carbon attributes of different energy resources in setting transmission rates for the sale of energy in interstate wholesale power markets. (Ch. 23)
- FERC should adopt a rule that clarifies the Public Utility Regulatory Policies Act's (PURPA's) application to non-dispatchable resources such as solar and wind, and should avoid granting broad waivers to PURPA mandatory buyback and avoided cost obligations based on a lack of utility market power where market failures impede renewable power projects from having access to competitive interstate markets. (Ch. 23)
- FERC should clarify the continued permissibility of state clean energy incentives and subsidies unless FERC expressly preempts them in a specific context (e.g., via adjudicative order or adoption of a notice-and-comment rule). (Ch. 23)
- FERC should issue a policy statement finding that interconnections for renewable power facilities presumptively meet the agency's public interest standard, and clarify how its nondiscrimination standard under §§205 and 206 of the Federal Power Act (which require the agency to

set just, reasonable, and nondiscriminatory rates) will apply to a decarbonized grid. (Ch. 23)

- FERC can require that wholesale rates include a carbon adder set at a level intended to reflect the social cost of carbon. (Ch. 24)
- FERC should consider the possibility of stranded assets when assessing proposals for fossil fuel infrastructure that will be paid for by ratepayers. (Ch. 24 and Ch. 24 App. B)
- FERC should require pipeline operators seeking to apply stricter quality standards to renewable gas than natural gas to provide a valid justification for that choice. (Ch. 26)
- FERC should adopt a policy statement calling for a higher rate of return on the equity investment in pipelines that are dedicated to the delivery of ethanol and biofuels. (Ch. 27)

U.S. Department of Agriculture (USDA)

- USDA should redeploy funding for biofuels research to development of fuels that have high-value uses, such as biomass-based diesel. (Ch. 27)
- USDA should ensure that government financial incentive and regulatory programs do not support large-scale operations without also requiring them to curb their most environmentally damaging practices (Ch. 30)
- USDA should develop and promote a national climate friendly wood product certification system analogous to its system for certifying organic produce. (Ch. 31)

U.S. Department of State

- The U.S. Department of State and U.S. Trade Representative should further a (preferably federal) decarbonization strategy tied to climate change mitigation and clean energy strategies when negotiating preferential trade agreements. (Ch. 8)
- The U.S. Department of State should play a lead role in addressing border tax adjustments and other decarbonization strategies within the negotiation phase of preferential trade agreements, particularly regional and plurilateral agreements. (Ch. 8)

- The U.S. Department of State should take a lead role in negotiating multilateral agreements concerning climate change that include decarbonization labeling standards. (Ch. 8)
- The U.S. Department of State should issue an interpretation of the air service agreements to state explicitly that the United States interprets "on the basis of reciprocity" to mean that either Party to the international air service agreement can start taxing international aviation fuel at any time. (Ch. 16)

Other Federal Agencies & Departments

- The Federal Highway Administration should launch a pilot program to facilitate the making of energy efficient mortgages and rehabilitation mortgages at interest rates below the market rate for standard home mortgage loans. (Ch. 11)
- The Federal Aviation Administration should reconsider its guidelines on state aviation taxes and redesign them to allow states to adopt appropriate taxes to reduce aviation emissions. (Ch. 16)
- The Bureau of Ocean Energy Management should continue its designation of wind energy areas, and prepare programmatic environmental impact statement to expedite approval of projects in those areas. (Ch. 18)
- The Council on Environmental Quality should amend its National Environmental Policy Act (NEPA) regulations to provide that a mitigated finding of no significant action is the preferred method for reviewing certain kinds of renewable projects if specified types of mitigation measures are undertaken and if the particular site does not pose special problems. (Ch. 18)
- The U.S. Fish & Wildlife Service could develop standard methodologies under the Endangered Species Act for mitigation of harms from particular kinds of utility-scale projects. (Ch. 18)
- The Nuclear Regulatory Commission should—consistent with the Atomic Energy Act and NEPA—eliminate contested hearings on NEPA issues (or at least move them forward in the process). (Ch. 21)
- The Department of the Interior should hat federal leasing of federal lands and waters for fossil fuel extraction. (Ch. 24 App. B)

- The Pipeline and Hazardous Materials Safety Administration should adopt more stringent repair requirements for renewable gas pipelines to minimize pipeline leaks and associated costs. (Ch. 26)
- BLM should enforce lease provisions that require ranchers to uphold conservation values, and add new ones designed to reduce the climate impacts of grazing systems. (Ch. 30)
- BLM should undertake a process to update the grazing intensity limit in leases to reflect current conditions, including range quality, climate, and animal size. (Ch. 30)
- The Federal Crop Insurance Corporation should require publicly funded crop insurance policies to treat greenhouse gas-intensive practices as risk enhancing and reduce or eliminate their premium subsidies accordingly. (Ch. 30)
- The Natural Resources Conservation Service should revise the Conservation Stewardship Program to prioritize low-carbon practices and to create a funding pool for farmers transitioning to, or practicing, carbon farming. (Ch. 30)
- The Risk Management Agency should ensure that its crop insurance policies do not interfere with cover cropping or other proven decarbonizing practices or conversely encourage less beneficial practices. (Ch. 30)

States and State Governments

- State governments should assess all near-term decisions against long-term goals and viable pathways to achieve them, balancing replacing retiring fossil fuel based infrastructure with available low-carbon technologies, in order to help minimize carbon lock-in and stranded assets. (Ch. 1)
- State governments should engage in integrated planning based on the efficient and transparent sharing of information between stakeholders, many of whom have not historically coordinated their efforts. (Ch. 1)
- State governments should address generational-scale lifestyle changes in two ways: playing offense, particularly when policymakers confront forks in the road where some lifestyle shifts could facilitate deep decarbonization, and playing defense by heading off lifestyle shifts that could undermine deep decarbonization. (Ch. 3)

- State governments should adopt and implement policy measures to reduce demand for energy services, not just to reduce the energy needed to supply those services. (Ch. 3)
- State governments should adopt and implement specific strategies that target increased uptake of more energy-efficient home equipment technologies, including green leases and improved life-cycle cost information for retailers and householders. (Ch. 3)
- State governments should consider using specific strategies to increase adoption of household-level renewable energy systems and purchases of products with low life-cycle emissions, such as informal marketing through neighborhoods and social networks and targeted marketing to environmentally minded consumers. (Ch. 3)
- State governments should further use, test, and evaluate specific strategies for motor vehicle efficiency, including improved energy labeling and vehicle fleet buyers' use of supply chain pressure. (Ch. 3)
- State governments should further use, test, and evaluate specific strategies to increase the uptake of energy-efficient buildings, including energy audits of existing homes and energy rating systems for new homes. (Ch. 3)
- State governments should further use, test, and evaluate specific strategies to reduce carbon emissions from the use of existing and new home equipment and buildings, including provision of monthly feedback and implementation of information campaigns. (Ch. 3)
- State governments should further use, test, and evaluate strategies for reducing carbon emissions from the use of existing and new motor vehicles and other forms of transportation, including provision of immediate fuel use feedback devices and development of eco-driving education programs. (Ch. 3)
- State governments should coordinate with federal and local governments, as well as corporations and businesses, to carefully plan technological change inducement programs. (Ch. 4)
- Assuming that the production tax credit will not continue past its phaseout date, state governments should assess the need for new incentives, similar to a production tax credit, which would permit continued growth for renewable technologies. (Ch. 5)

- More states should assess the benefits of a comprehensive renewable energy plan that takes into account multiple stakeholders (i.e., cost to consumer, grid integration, and private investment). (Ch. 5)
- State governments should support financing of carbon reducing technologies through the issuance of green bonds. (Ch. 5)
- State governments should work together with the federal government and the private sector to study and understand the effects that incentives like the production tax credit have on the growth of renewable technologies. (Ch. 5)
- State governments should work with the federal government and the private sector to continually assess and adjust incentives like the investment tax credit in order to promote the advancement of new technologies. (Ch. 5)
- States should consider adopting and implementing programs similar to Texas' "competitive renewable energy zones" program that are directed at improving and expanding transmission infrastructure. (Ch. 5)
- States and larger localities or regions should establish green banks or similar Sustainable Finance Organizations. (Ch. 6)
- States should assure that each community is entitled to act as an aggregator of energy and energy services provided by its citizens with the same rights to deliver wholesale energy and energy services as its citizens. (Ch. 6)
- States should assure that each community is entitled to prompt, convenient access to aggregate information gathered by public utilities about their citizens' energy use and the energy services the citizens deliver. (Ch. 6)
- States should assure that each community may purchase or generate energy on behalf of its citizens directly or through contractual arrangements with third parties. (Ch. 6)
- States should assure that each energy customer is entitled to grid access on a nondiscriminatory basis to provide wholesale energy and energy services through open, transparent markets or at just and reasonable rates to the local distribution company. (Ch. 6)

- States should assure that each energy customer is entitled to prompt, convenient access to all information gathered by public utilities regarding its own energy use and energy services it delivers. (Ch. 6)
- States should assure that each energy customer may generate and manage energy behind its meter and contract with third parties to assist them in doing so. (Ch. 6)
- States should assure that each energy customer may purchase clean energy from local energy providers through its own or the provider's distribution system. (Ch. 6)
- States should assure that each energy customer may purchase energy through local group or community arrangements. (Ch. 6)
- Wherever a state government has jurisdiction over an energy project participant, it should use its authority to require reporting of carbon performance information on an ongoing basis. (Ch. 6)
- States could adopt laws with more ambitious goals (e.g., zero waste), intermediate targets and timetables for achieving these more ambitious goals, and means of achieving them. (Ch. 7)
- States should adopt laws that other states have adopted on the waste problems posed by products, packaging, food scraps, and industrial waste. (Ch. 7)
- State governments must adopt decarbonization laws that comply with international trade rules. (Ch. 8)
- State governments should avoid adopting decarbonization laws that contain local content requirements. (Ch. 8)
- If a state government designs a decarbonization law that contains local content requirements, it should meet the national treatment requirements under Article III of the General Agreement on Tariffs and Trade. (Ch. 8)
- State governments should consider feed-in tariffs as long as they comply with applicable trade rules. (Ch. 8)
- States should structure decarbonization labeling schemes so as not to discriminate against foreign imports. (Ch. 8)

- States should adopt an energy-efficiency resource standard set at an initial ambitious level and periodically reexamine and strengthen the savings level as more-efficient technologies evolve. (Ch. 9)
- States should adopt appropriate policies to align utility business models with energy efficiency investments, make utilities whole for energy efficiency programs, and provide incentives for strong energy efficiency performance. (Ch. 9)
- States should allow utilities to recover the prudently incurred costs of energy-efficiency programs. (Ch. 9)
- States should consider adopting legislation and programs that encourage the use of energy-efficient appliances and equipment through tax policy, financial incentives, labeling programs, and financing policies. (Ch. 9)
- States should consider performance-based ratemaking designs that include incentives for superior utility energy-efficiency performance. (Ch. 9)
- States should develop an integrated suite of energy efficiency policies that combine, co-ordinate, and synthesize a full suite of complementary energy efficiency policies, including mandatory minimum energy efficiency standards, voluntary labeling and incentive programs that further increase produce energy efficiency levels over time, tax incentives, and other complementary energy efficiency policies that are part of a larger set of decarbonization policies. (Ch. 9)
- States should enact laws requiring that building owners who presently use fossil fuel for space and water heating must retrofit their buildings by electrification if a federal mandatory law is not obtainable. (Ch. 11)
- States should require an energy audit upon the sale or rental of existing homes and commercial properties if the federal government fails to do so. (Ch. 11)
- State governments should adopt measures to send better price signals regarding the cost of driving, including increased motor fuel taxes. (Ch. 13)
- State governments should devote a larger share of transportation funding to providing meaningful alternatives to driving, and increase fund-

ing for projects that better connect various modes in order to expand transportation choices. (Ch. 13)

- State governments should pursue reforms that better link transportation and land use, including targeting transportation funding and planning resources to encourage transit-oriented development. (Ch. 13)
- States should add greenhouse gas assessment to their transportation planning laws and policies and reorient transportation planning to advance decarbonization. (Ch. 13)
- State governments can call upon current alternative vehicle owners to educate potential consumers about alternative fuel vehicles. (Ch. 14)
- State governments should allocate funding and institute regulations to incentivize electric vehicle charging in residential spaces. (Ch. 14)
- State governments should assist in research and development toward the goal of reducing battery costs. (Ch. 14)
- State governments should consider prioritizing support for expanding the faster growing market (i.e., electric vehicles), rather than trying to promote a lagging hydrogen fuel cell vehicle market. (Ch. 14)
- State governments should create programs to train electric vehicle employees. (Ch. 14)
- State governments should proactively address safety standards, regulations, and liability regimes for autonomous vehicles. (Ch. 14)
- States should consider providing incentives to encourage owners of multiunit dwellings to add access to electrical outlets in parking areas. (Ch. 14)
- States should establish programs and regulations to facilitate residential charging infrastructure. (Ch. 14)
- States could formulate their own greenhouse gas standards for shipping and submit them to the U.S. Environmental Protection Agency (EPA) for approval or, alternatively, set in-use requirements without EPA approval. (Ch. 17)
- States should enact statutes to prohibit state officials and local governments from banning renewable energy facilities and require state offi-

cials and local governments to make decisions in facility siting within a reasonable period of time. (Ch. 18)

- States with offshore wind capacity should develop and implement processes to promptly review and act upon applications for offshore wind projects. (Ch. 18)
- States without adequate laws and procedures in place to review and approve large-scale renewable projects should adopt such laws. (Ch. 18)
- State governments should provide incentives for planned communities to install district heating infrastructure in newly built or remodeled mixed-use zones so that residential construction could take advantage of waste heat. (Ch. 19)
- States should enact statewide building mandates for zero net energy (ZNE) buildings and include the self-generation portion of ZNE buildings in the mandates. (Ch. 19)
- States should include in their renewable portfolio standard mandates (1) solar energy, specifically from distributed generation sources, (2) energy storage and microgrid capacity, and (3) thermal energy systems that can contribute to decarbonization. (Ch. 19)
- States can fund additional research, technology, and development on a range of distribution network and smart grid developments, including energy storage. (Ch. 20)
- States should adopt new laws or regulatory policies to create additional flexibility for how to classify energy storage projects for purposes of ratepayer recovery, or other means of rewarding energy storage initiatives, to facilitate greater integration of renewable energy into the grid. (Ch. 20)
- States should continue and then complete ongoing efforts to fully value the benefits of nuclear power, including consideration of zero emissions credit programs. (Ch. 21)
- States should consider including pumped storage hydro as transmission assets entitled to cost-of-service rate recovery in their transmission planning as an alternative to construction of new transmission lines. (Ch. 22)

- State regulators could consider more flexible cost recovery tools that allow utilities to take advantage of the passage of time, including subjecting project approvals to ongoing prudence review to recognize new information about different technologies and project construction costs. (Ch. 23)
- States should adopt incentives that enable customer behavior/investment choices, including decoupling, customer demand response, and deployment of smart metering. (Ch. 23)
- States should evaluate new power projects based on their system-wide project costs and benefits, and should favor integrated planning approaches that compare the social costs and benefits of various power projects. (Ch. 23)
- State governments could pay utilities the remaining "book value" for investor utility-owned plants, and negotiate prices with private plant owners to pay them to close greenhouse gas-emitting facilities. (Ch. 24)
- State governments should require companies to consider the possibility that their fossil fuel-related assets would be stranded, before making investment decisions. (Ch. 24)
- States could ban or limit coal mining and oil and gas production. (Ch. 24)
- States could impose an outright ban on new coal-fired generation and/or a formal limit on new natural gas generation additions. (Ch. 24)
- States could put a limit on greenhouse gas emissions related to power generation. (Ch. 24)
- States could require utility planners to include a carbon adder for planning purposes. (Ch. 24)
- States with explicit climate policies should insist that utility resource plans reflect a reasonable schedule for ramping down the use of fossil-fired generation. (Ch. 24)
- States without explicit climate policies should rely on their obligation to ensure that utility rates are just and reasonable to require that resource plans reflect stiffer greenhouse gas restrictions that may apply in the years ahead. (Ch. 24)

- States should expand climate change planning and modeling to: (1) analyze what it would take to make workers and regions dependent on carbon jobs whole; and (2) develop plans to achieve a level of equity and "shared prosperity" that would unite community members behind a common battle to reduce carbon emissions. (Ch. 24 App. A)
- States should adopt or expand programs aimed at greenhouse gas emissions mitigation or sequestration from the forestry or agricultural sectors. (Ch. 25)
- States should adopt policies to keep forests from being converted to cropland, keep natural and biodiverse forests from being converted to biofuel forests, increase carbon sink potential of agricultural soils by forestalling conversion to more carbon-intensive uses, and protect watersheds and biodiversity from natural resource conversion related to residential, industrial, and commercial development. (Ch. 25)
- States should consider implementing policies aimed at more stringently regulating, preserving, and expanding forest lands. (Ch. 25)
- States should consider adopting renewable portfolio standards for gas, requiring a minimum percentage of total supply to be met with biogas, hydrogen, and/or synthetic methane. (Ch. 26)
- States should enact legislation designating a single agency with responsibility for issuing all necessary permits for renewable gas production facilities. (Ch. 26)
- State governors could issue executive orders to (1) direct agencies to purchase a minimum amount of CCS-produced energy; and (2) significantly raise the minimum total amount of clean energy to be purchased by the state government by 2050, where the grid includes plants that are or can be equipped with CCS. (Ch. 28)
- States and/or regions could form and fund agencies akin to public utilities to conduct siting analyses, acquire property access rights, and otherwise coordinate and facilitate expansion of the carbon dioxide pipeline network. (Ch. 28)
- States can impose restrictions on carbon dioxide emissions to drive carbon capture and sequestration (CCS). For example, states can adopt carbon emissions standards on new sources that require full CCS on new coal-fired units by the early 2020s, and partial and full CCS on

new natural gas combined cycle (NGCC) units by the mid-2020s and early 2030s, respectively. (Ch. 28)

- States could expand their renewable portfolio standard laws to become clean energy standards, mandating not just the purchase of renewable energy, but also energy produced by coal-fired and natural gas combined-cycle NGCC plants that are equipped to capture carbon dioxide. (Ch. 28)
- State governments can reduce barriers to negative emissions technologies from legal requirements, environmental permitting requirements, or environmental impact reviews in a manner that will not expose the public or the environment to unwarranted environmental risks. (Ch. 29)
- State governments should consider the designation of carbon removal technologies as an accepted method to attain renewable portfolio standard targets. (Ch. 29)
- State governments should consider requiring farm owners to comply with basic climate-friendly practices, such as installing buffer strips next to streams, in order to receive tax benefits for agricultural activities or easements. (Ch. 30)
- States should adopt legislation banning food waste in landfills, using Vermont's Universal Recycling Law as a model. (Ch. 30)
- State governments should expand publicly owned forests by acquiring and reforesting private lands, focusing on lands rendered economically unproductive by the effects of climate change. (Ch. 31)
- California should continue to use its ability to enact and strengthen state mobile source standards. (Ch. 32)
- If EPA changes its approach of deferring to California when reviewing waiver requests, California should vigorously protect the California waiver by suing EPA. (Ch. 32)
- Other states should adopt California emission standards and work closely with California to identify priorities for future standards, identify the local benefits of adopting the California standards, and expose the risks of delaying action. (Ch. 32)

- States should develop and implement transportation plans that are designed to achieve zero emission transportation systems. (Ch. 32)
- States should develop comprehensive woodstove replacement programs, accompanied by funding necessary to enable low-income access to modern technologies, to accelerate turnover. (Ch. 32)
- States should enact indirect source rules to limit the extent to which stationary sources attract and encourage mobile source emissions. (Ch. 32)
- State governments should update and amend their green purchasing program requirements to eliminate purchases of hydrofluorocarbon (HFC)-containing equipment where other low-global warming potential and more energy-efficient alternatives are available on the market. (Ch. 34)
- State governments should use life-cycle climate performance accounting in their energy efficiency programs and regulations. (Ch. 34)
- State governors should adopt executive orders mandating that state and local government agencies identify measures to reduce HFC emissions. (Ch. 34)
- States could work collaboratively to issue collective standards for life-cycle climate performance on consumer appliances for which no federal standard has been issued. (Ch. 34)

State Agencies (see also Utilities, State Public Utility Commissions)

- State environmental agencies should require measurement and verification metering and supervisory control and data acquisition devices that permit accurate measurement of energy savings and carbon performance from utility energy efficiency programs. (Ch. 6)
- State education agencies should provide training opportunities to builders, architects, developers, and others through community colleges, universities, vocational technical schools, and other educational institutions on high-efficiency and zero-energy building construction practices, as well as passive solar techniques. (Ch. 10)
- State agencies should amend their rules to specifically address the permitting of renewable gas production facilities. (Ch. 26)

- State environmental agencies can adopt: (1) standardized approval and review procedures for negative emissions technologies (NETs) that use common procedures or similar physical designs; and (2) general permits for NETs that will likely have either small or predictable and controlled impacts to the environment. (Ch. 29)
- State environmental agencies could promote the reuse of captured carbon dioxide as a feedstock or commercial product by issuing guidance or a regulatory determination that carbon dioxide captured through NETs would not constitute a pollutant or waste under other federal environmental statutes if reused. (Ch. 29)
- State foresters should use existing authority to recognize the importance of considering carbon capture, geologic sequestration and climate change adaptation in management decisions regarding state forests. (Ch. 31)
- State land management agencies should develop prescribed burn protocols and land management strategies to minimize the net warming caused by emissions of fine particulate matter and carbon dioxide. (Ch. 32)
- State agricultural agencies should invest in technical support programs aimed at educating farmers about "win-win" measures—specifically, management strategies that improve nitrogen use efficiency, reduce fertilizer requirements, and reduce nitrous oxide emissions. (Ch. 35)
- State environmental authorities should seek to regulate nitrous oxide emissions from agriculture and livestock through management standards, rather than direct emission caps, due to the complexities of monitoring, verifying, and enforcing compliance with emissions caps for these sectors. (Ch. 35)
- When designing and implementing cap-and-trade programs, state regulators should incentivize nitrous oxide emission reductions from agricultural and livestock sources by providing offset credit for such reductions. (Ch. 35)

State Legislatures

- State legislatures should adopt long-term tax incentives that take into account the life of carbon-reducing energy projects in order to allow stakeholders to plan investments and growth for the future. (Ch. 5)

- State legislatures should act to allow subsidy funds to be combined with private finance to create low-income housing rehabilitation programs that require energy-efficiency standards be met in the rehabilitation process. (Ch. 6)
- State legislatures should continue to use subsidies (preferably without local content requirements) in the form of tax credits, accelerated depreciation, or cash grants, in combination with other incentives, to help create a market for renewable energy that would eventually drive down some of the production costs. (Ch. 8)
- If a state legislature decides to adopt a local content requirement for decarbonization, it could limit the requirement to government procurement, particularly if it is linked to decarbonization policies or protection of public health. (Ch. 8)
- States legislatures should adopt utility rate designs that align utility interests with energy efficiency, such as decoupling. (Ch. 9)
- State legislatures or governors should establish state zero-energy building goals, such as California's goals under California's Building Energy Efficiency Standards. (Ch. 10)
- State legislatures should adopt a price for carbon either through a carbon tax or through cap-and-trade systems that include new buildings. (Ch. 10)
- State legislatures should follow the lead of states like California, Hawaii, and Washington in developing advanced building and energy codes that significantly reduce the energy used by new buildings. (Ch. 10)
- State legislatures should maintain or adopt laws such as renewable portfolio standards, net metering, cost of solar tariffs, and renewable energy tax credits that encourage more rapid integration of renewable energy into the grid, thereby facilitating the goal of low-carbon electrification of new buildings. (Ch. 10)
- State legislatures should adopt mandatory retrofit laws for energy conservation and decarbonization in existing commercial and residential buildings if the federal government does not do so. (Ch. 11)
- State legislatures should continue to expand financial and other support infrastructure for expanded use of electric vehicles. (Ch. 14)

- State legislatures should use pay-as-you-drive, vehicle miles traveled options, or a one-time fee charged to electric vehicle owners at the time of registration, to help ensure that alternative vehicles contribute their share to road construction and maintenance. (Ch. 14)
- State legislatures should enact laws to recognize and protect the right of landowners to install and operate solar technologies on their properties without significant restrictions. (Ch. 19)
- State legislatures should expand community solar ownership legislation, such as virtual net metering, for all customers. (Ch. 19)
- State legislatures should facilitate the deployment of solar installations through third party ownership models and community solar ownership legislation, such as virtual net metering, for all customers. (Ch. 19)
- State legislatures should help cut costs of deploying all distributed generation thermal technologies by standardizing permitting costs and creating uniform processes. (Ch. 19)
- State legislatures could amend existing laws to direct their state public utility commissions to consider regional and national need as well as clean energy goals in determining whether there is a "need" for a transmission line that will impact the state. (Ch. 20)
- State legislatures could make clear that merchant transmission line companies can seek siting permits and exercise eminent domain authority under the same conditions as electric utilities. (Ch. 20)
- To the extent state law sets out what is a "public use" for purposes of eminent domain authority, state legislatures could amend the law to make clear that public use includes benefits to a multi-state region as well as to the individual state. (Ch. 20)
- State legislatures could impose a nuclear portfolio standard that would co-exist alongside existing renewable portfolio standards or broaden the scope of existing renewable portfolio standards to incorporate all "clean" energy, including nuclear power. (Ch. 21)
- States legislatures should encourage local governments to take initiative in building clean energy infrastructure, especially to the extent that this allows them to draw on tax-free financing options. (Ch. 23)

- State legislatures could allow utilities to charge ratepayers for the cost of industrywide hiring halls and for retraining that bridges the gap between workers' old skills and new occupations. (Ch. 24 App. A)
- State legislatures could require wind, solar, or energy efficiency companies to give hiring preference to displaced coal or coal-fired utility workers within future renewable energy portfolio standards or energy efficiency mandates, while also establishing wage standards that improve job quality in renewable and energy efficiency jobs. (Ch. 24 App. A)
- State legislatures should promote the creation of more clean energy jobs in coal country. (Ch. 24 App. A)
- State legislatures could adjust commercial forest management programs to more directly integrate deep decarbonization objectives, particularly related to regeneration, regulation (or prevention) of conversion of feedstock forests to other, non-forested uses, and regulation of greenhouse gas-emitting technology utilized during the feedstock cultivation process. (Ch. 25)
- State legislatures should designate a lead agency with responsibility for coordinating the various permitting processes for renewable gas gathering pipelines. (Ch. 26)
- State legislatures could provide tax credits or grant funding to stimulate investment in research and development focused on the costs and benefits of pre-transport processing of feedstocks. (Ch. 27)
- State legislatures should adopt measures that would stimulate investment in barge and rail transport—such as tax incentives or additional public investment in intermodal facilities—to allow increased use of rail transport for feedstock production. (Ch. 27)
- State legislatures should adopt measures that would stimulate investment in biofuels receiving terminals—such as tax incentives or grants for eligible terminal improvements—to facilitate increased use of rail transport for biofuels delivery. (Ch. 27)
- State legislatures should include combined heat and power in their state renewable portfolio standard or energy efficiency resource standards. (Ch. 27)

- State legislatures should provide incentives to encourage the construction of pipelines that are dedicated to the delivery of ethanol and biofuels. (Ch. 27)
- To achieve carbon dioxide removal at the necessary scale within a relevant time frame, state legislatures should significantly boost the funding available to support negative emissions technology research proposals. (Ch. 29)
- State legislatures should consider adopting a fertilizer fee that could both encourage more judicious use of fertilizer and help fund training on how to ensure no yield losses with less fertilizer and other climate-friendly agricultural practices. (Ch. 30)
- State legislatures should amend state forestry laws to recognize the importance of considering carbon capture and climate change adaptation in management decisions regarding state forests. (Ch. 31)
- State legislatures should consider a modest carbon tax or greenhouse gas cap-and-trade program that recognizes private forest carbon capture as an emission offset, exempts emissions from sustainably produced biomass, and also imposes a tax burden on those who deforest their land through conversion. (Ch. 31)
- State legislatures should adopt legislation mandating that state and local government agencies identify measures to reduce hydrofluorocarbon emissions. (Ch. 34)

Local Governments

- Local governments should assess all near-term decisions against long-term goals and viable pathways to achieve them, balancing replacing retiring fossil fuel based infrastructure with available low-carbon technologies, in order to help minimize carbon lock-in and stranded assets. (Ch. 1)
- Local governments should engage in integrated planning based on the efficient and transparent sharing of information between stakeholders, many of whom have not historically coordinated their efforts. (Ch. 1)
- Local governments should address generational-scale lifestyle changes in two ways: playing offense, particularly when policymakers confront forks in the road where some lifestyle shifts could facilitate deep

decarbonization, and playing defense by heading off lifestyle shifts that could undermine deep decarbonization. (Ch. 3)

- Local governments should adopt and implement policy measures to reduce demand for energy services, not just to reduce the energy needed to supply those services. (Ch. 3)
- Local governments should adopt and implement specific strategies that target increased uptake of more energy-efficient home equipment technologies, including green leases and improved life-cycle cost information for retailers and householders. (Ch. 3)
- Local governments should consider using specific strategies to increase adoption of household-level renewable energy systems and purchases of products with low life-cycle emissions, such as informal marketing through neighborhoods and social networks and targeted marketing to environmentally minded consumers. (Ch. 3)
- Local governments should further use, test, and evaluate specific strategies for motor vehicle efficiency, including improved energy labeling and vehicle fleet buyers' use of supply chain pressure. (Ch. 3)
- Local governments should further use, test, and evaluate specific strategies to increase the uptake of energy-efficient buildings, including energy audits of existing homes and energy rating systems for new homes. (Ch. 3)
- Local governments should further use, test, and evaluate specific strategies to reduce carbon emissions from the use of existing and new home equipment and buildings, including provision of monthly feedback and implementation of information campaigns. (Ch.3)
- Local governments should further use, test, and evaluate strategies for reducing carbon emissions from the use of existing and new motor vehicles and other forms of transportation, including provision of immediate fuel use feedback devices and development of eco-driving education programs. (Ch. 3)
- Local governments should coordinate with federal and state governments, as well as corporations and businesses, to carefully plan technological change inducement programs. (Ch. 4)
- Local governments should support financing of carbon reducing technologies through the issuance of green bonds. (Ch. 5)

- More local governments should assess the benefits of a comprehensive renewable energy plan that takes into account multiple stakeholders (i.e., cost to consumer, grid integration, and private investment). (Ch. 5)
- Wherever a local government has jurisdiction over an energy project participant, it should use its authority to require reporting of carbon performance information on an ongoing basis. (Ch. 6)
- Local governments could adopt laws with more ambitious goals (e.g., zero waste), intermediate targets and timetables for achieving these more ambitious goals, and means of achieving them. (Ch. 7)
- Local governments should adopt laws that other local governments have adopted on the waste problems posed by products, packaging, food scraps, and industrial waste. (Ch. 7)
- Local governments must adopt decarbonization laws that comply with international trade rules. (Ch. 8)
- Local governments should avoid adopting decarbonization laws that contain local content requirements. (Ch. 8)
- If a local government designs a decarbonization law that contains local content requirements, it should meet the national treatment requirements under Article III of the General Agreement on Tariffs and Trade. (Ch. 8)
- If a local legislature decides to adopt a local content requirement for decarbonization, it could limit the the requirement to government procurement, particularly if it is linked to decarbonization policies or protection of public health. (Ch. 8)
- All cities should consider adoption of benchmarking ordinances, as well as energy audit and energy savings implementation measures. (Ch. 9)
- Cities should adopt and fully enforce city building energy-efficiency codes (unless preempted by state law). (Ch. 9)
- Cities should develop an integrated suite of energy efficiency policies that combine, co-ordinate, and synthesize a full suite of complementary energy efficiency policies, including mandatory minimum energy efficiency standards, voluntary labeling and incentive programs that further increase produce energy efficiency levels over time, tax incen-

tives, and other complementary energy efficiency policies that are part of a larger set of decarbonization policies. (Ch. 9)

- Cities should establish city tax deductions or credits for the purchase of energy-efficient equipment. (Ch. 9)
- Cities should establish financing programs for energy efficiency. (Ch. 9)
- Local legislative bodies should require energy use disclosures for larger commercial buildings (e.g., buildings larger than 50,000 square feet and multifamily buildings), and require benchmarking information to be made publicly available in a format that is easy to understand so that it can be readily used in rental and purchase decisions. (Ch. 10)
- Within the authority granted to them under state law and state building code requirements, local legislative bodies should adopt advanced building and energy codes that drive down carbon use in buildings. (Ch. 10)
- Local governments should expand publicly owned forests by acquiring and reforesting private lands, focusing on lands rendered economically unproductive by the effects of climate change. (Ch. 13)
- Localities should alter or eliminate sprawl-inducing zoning provisions, such as minimum lot and house sizes, and revamp zoning and building code requirements to promote more compact, mixed-use development. (Ch. 13)
- Localities should eliminate free on-street parking, raise parking rates (and consider demand-based parking prices that change to maintain a certain percentage of vacant spaces), and amend zoning regulations to trim the amount of free parking developers are required to provide. (Ch. 13)
- Localities should pursue reforms that better link transportation and land use, including targeting transportation funding and planning resources to encourage transit-oriented development. (Ch. 13)
- Metropolitan planning organizations should include greenhouse gas assessment in their policies and reorient transportation planning to advance decarbonization. (Ch. 13)
- Cities should establish programs and regulations to facilitate residential charging infrastructure. Local government incentives should encour-

age owners of multiunit dwellings to add access to electrical outlets in parking areas. (Ch. 14)

- Local governments can call upon current alternative vehicle owners to educate potential consumers about alternative fuel vehicles. (Ch. 14)
- Local governments should allocate funding and institute regulations to incentivize electric vehicle charging in residential spaces. (Ch. 14)
- Local governments should assist in research and development toward the goal of reducing battery costs. (Ch. 14)
- Local governments should consider prioritizing support for expanding the faster growing market (i.e., electric vehicles), rather than trying to promote a lagging hydrogen fuel cell vehicle market. (Ch. 14)
- Local governments should continue to expand financial and other support infrastructure for expanded use of electric vehicles. (Ch. 14)
- Local governments should proactively address safety standards, regulations, and liability regimes for autonomous vehicles. (Ch. 14)
- Local governments should increase investment in freight transportation infrastructure. (Ch. 15)
- Local governments should educate those involved in their tree planting campaigns about the impacts tree shadows can have on distributed generation solar energy systems and provide guidance about how to pick tree species (e.g., those with lower maturation heights or those with less sun-blocking foliage or branches) and where to place them to minimize their negative impacts. (Ch. 19)
- Local governments should provide incentives for planned communities to install district heating infrastructure in newly built or remodeled mixed-use zones so that residential construction could take advantage of waste heat. (Ch. 19)
- Local governments should promote the creation of more clean energy jobs in coal country. (Ch. 24 App. A)
- Localities should expand climate change planning and modeling to: (1) analyze what it would take to make workers and regions dependent on carbon jobs whole; and (2) develop plans to achieve a level of equity and "shared prosperity" that would unite community members behind a common battle to reduce carbon emissions. (Ch. 24 App. A)

- Local zoning boards should amend their rules to specifically address the development of renewable gas production facilities, unless their definitions of industrial or manufacturing uses are already sufficiently broad. (Ch. 26)
- Local governments should adopt measures that would stimulate investment in barge and rail transport—such as tax incentives or additional public investment in intermodal facilities—to allow increased use of rail transport for feedstock production. (Ch.27)
- Local governments should adopt measures that would stimulate investment in biofuels receiving terminals—such as tax incentives or grants for eligible terminal improvements—to facilitate increased use of rail transport for biofuels delivery. (Ch. 27)
- Local governments, through their own purchasing, advertising, or public support, could also encourage a wider range of whole or minimally processed plant-based options, and other climate-friendly options, at restaurants. (Ch. 30)
- Local governments should enact in-use restrictions that prohibit idling of all vehicles, but particularly heavy-duty diesel vehicles. (Ch. 32)
- Local governments should update and amend their green purchasing program requirements to eliminate purchases of hydrofluorocarbon-containing equipment where other low-global warming potential and more energy-efficient alternatives are available on the market. (Ch. 34)
- Local governments should use life-cycle climate performance accounting in their energy efficiency programs and regulations. (Ch. 34)
- When designing and implementing cap-and-trade programs, regional authorities should incentivize nitrous oxide emission reductions from agricultural and livestock sources by providing offset credit for such reductions. (Ch. 35)

Companies, Associations, NGOs, and Other Private Entities

- Private actors should assess all near-term decisions against long-term goals and viable pathways to achieve them, balancing replacing retiring fossil fuel based infrastructure with available low-carbon technologies, in order to help minimize carbon lock-in and stranded assets. (Ch. 1)

- Private actors should engage in integrated planning based on the efficient and transparent sharing of information between stakeholders, many of whom have not historically coordinated their efforts, in order to successfully achieve deep decarbonization. (Ch. 1)
- Corporations and other private organizations should consider using specific strategies to increase adoption of household-level renewable energy systems and purchases of products with low life-cycle emissions, such as informal marketing through neighborhoods and social networks and targeted marketing to environmentally minded consumers. (Ch. 3)
- Corporations and other private organizations should further use, test, and evaluate specific strategies for motor vehicle efficiency, including improved energy labeling and vehicle fleet buyers' use of supply chain pressure. (Ch. 3)
- Corporations and other private organizations should further use, test, and evaluate specific strategies to increase the uptake of energy-efficient buildings, including energy audits of existing homes and energy rating systems for new homes. (Ch.3)
- Corporations and other private organizations should adopt and implement specific strategies that target the increased uptake of more energy-efficient home equipment, including green leases and improved life-cycle cost information for retailers and householders. (Ch. 3)
- Corporations and other private organizations should further use, test, and evaluate specific strategies to reduce carbon emissions from the use of existing and new home equipment and buildings, including provision of monthly feedback and implementation of information campaigns. (Ch. 3)
- Corporations and other private organizations should further use, test, and evaluate strategies for reducing carbon emissions from the operation of existing and new motor vehicles and other forms of transportation, including provision of immediate fuel use feedback devices and development of eco-driving education programs. (Ch. 3)
- Private-sector decisionmakers should address generational-scale lifestyle changes in two ways: playing offense, particularly when policymakers confront forks in the road where some lifestyle shifts could

facilitate deep decarbonization, and playing defense by heading off lifestyle shifts that could undermine deep decarbonization. (Ch. 3)

- Corporations and businesses should coordinate with federal, state, and local governments, as well as with other corporations and businesses, to carefully plan technological change inducement programs. (Ch. 4)
- The private sector should work with the federal government and state governments and the private sector to continually assess and adjust incentives like the investment tax credit in order to promote the advancement of new technologies. (Ch. 5)
- Building industry trade groups, lending industry trade groups, and nongovernmental organizations should work together to: (1) promote verifiable standards for new building energy efficiency; (2) insure that construction and real estate sales contracts for new buildings require testing and verification of energy performance; and (3) require building appraisals and mortgage credit evaluations to reflect building energy consumption. (Ch. 6)
- Sustainable finance organizations should require measurement and verification metering and supervisory control and data acquisition devices that permit accurate measurement of energy savings and carbon performance from utility energy efficiency programs. (Ch. 6)
- Companies that operate at every stage of economic activity—from extraction to transportation to manufacture to retail to service—should consider mechanisms, including circular economy concepts, through which they can demonstrate leadership in materials and solid waste management and reduce the use and waste of embedded greenhouse gas emissions. (Ch. 7)
- Corporations should create sustainability programs headed by high level management that commit them to reduce greenhouse gas emissions by at least 25%, improving energy efficiency of operations by at least 50%, and reducing electricity demand by at least 15%. (Ch. 9)
- Building owners should take full life-cycle costs and the carbon impacts of materials into account when deciding on the energy-efficiency measures for new buildings, with the aim of reducing embodied carbon and overall environmental impacts. (Ch. 10)

- Consistent with the American Institute of Architects' 2030 Challenge, building developers and purchasers should commit to building only zero-energy buildings by no later than 2030. (Ch. 10)
- The private sector should promote teleworking and telecommuting, and employ flexible and compressed work schedules to reduce peak travel and overall driving. (Ch. 13)
- Transportation network companies should expand and increase services that work in concert with low or zero emission transportation alternatives, including public transit, bicycling, walking, and the use of zero emission motor vehicles. (Ch. 13)
- Private actors should offer residential charging stations at apartment buildings and other locations. (Ch. 14)
- Private stakeholders should create programs to train electric vehicle employees. (Ch. 14)
- The private sector should assist in research and development toward the goal of reducing battery costs. (Ch. 14)
- The private sector should consider prioritizing support for expanding the faster growing market (i.e., electric vehicles), rather than trying to promote a lagging hydrogen fuel cell vehicle market. (Ch. 14)
- The private sector should enable or encourage less flying. (Ch. 16)
- Companies with high shipping volumes (e.g., Walmart, IKEA, Nike) could impose supply chain requirements, such as only moving their goods on ships that meet a certain efficiency standard, use a low-carbon fuel, or slow steam. (Ch. 17)
- Ports can differentiate port charges or fees based on greenhouse gas emissions of particular ships. (Ch. 17)
- Nongovernmental organizations should set ambitious goals, such as the 100% renewable energy goal, to maintain pressure on governments and corporations to make efforts to promote distributed generation resources. (Ch. 19)
- Nongovernmental organizations, such as nonprofits, should educate those involved in their tree planting campaigns about the impacts tree shadows can have on distributed generation solar energy systems and provide guidance about how to pick tree species (e.g., those with lower

maturation heights or those with less sun-blocking foliage or branches) and where to place them to minimize their negative impacts. (Ch. 19)

- Transmission line companies should hold community meetings early and often, partner with environmental groups, create local construction partners, and provide direct tax benefits to local communities as well as voluntary payments to the communities on a per-mile basis to reduce opposition to transmission lines. (Ch. 20)
- Auto manufacturers can call upon current alternative vehicle owners to educate potential consumers about alternate fuel vehicles. (Ch. 24)
- Regional planners, which consist of transmission owners and grid operators in a specific geographical area, should consider what it would take to phase out the use of fossil-fired generation and prepare to meet long-term greenhouse gas reduction goals. (Ch. 24)
- Fossil fuel companies should, in their securities filings and other disclosures, provide detailed discussions of: (1) how their businesses would transition to a carbon pricing or regulatory system that is consistent with a two degree world; and (2) what will happen to their businesses and physical assets of the world fails to keep temperatures within two degrees above pre-industrial conditions. (Ch. 24 App. B)
- Wind, solar, or energy efficiency companies should give hiring preference to displaced coal or coal-fired utility workers; state legislatures could require this within future renewable energy portfolio standards or energy efficiency mandates, while also establishing wage standards that improve job quality in renewable and energy efficiency jobs. (Ch. 24 App. A)
- Agricultural land trusts should incorporate climate change mitigation into easement purposes, ensuring that easement conditions encourage climate-friendly practices and that farmers' efforts to mitigate climate change do not conflict with their easements. (Ch. 30)
- The American Forest and Paper Association should include in its Sustainable Forestry Initiative certification program standards maximizing the potential for forestry carbon capture and sequestration (CCS). (Ch. 31)

- The Forest Stewardship Council should include in its sustainable forestry certification program standards maximizing the potential for forestry CCS. (Ch. 31)
- Standards and code-making bodies should continue research and testing for all sectors to ensure the rapid and safe deployment of new low-global warming potential cooling and refrigeration technologies and equipment. (Ch. 34)
- The U.S. Green Building Council could amend the Leadership in Energy and Environmental Design certification to make the use of low-global warming potential refrigerants and high energy efficiency prerequisites for qualifying for credit. (Ch. 34)

Public Utilities

- Electric utilities should adopt or expand voluntary home energy audit programs. (Ch. 11)
- Utilities can help to ensure that electric vehicle (EV) customers charge at optimal times by experimenting with different incentive structures that encourage off-peak charging. (Ch. 14)
- Utilities should also incorporate the demand from EVs in their load forecasts and integrated resource plans and look to EVs to ease the flat and declining demand curve projections for electricity. (Ch. 14)
- Utilities should consider allowing ratepayers' vehicles to charge during low-demand times and discharge the power back to the grid during peak times, serving as forms of grid batteries. (Ch. 14)
- Utilities should educate those involved in their tree planting campaigns about the impacts tree shadows can have on distributed generation solar energy systems and provide guidance about how to pick tree species (e.g., those with lower maturation heights or those with less sun-blocking foliage or branches) and where to place them to minimize their negative impacts. (Ch. 19)
- Municipal utilities and electric cooperatives should divest ownership of their coal-fired generating units. (Ch. 24)

- Retail utilities should develop "standard offer programs" that would stimulate investment in distributed energy resources—and combined heat and power in particular—for industrial customers, including biorefineries. (Ch. 27)
- Utilities should include low-global warming potential refrigerants in their energy efficiency incentive programs. (Ch. 34)

Regional Transmission Organizations (RTOs)/Independant System Operators (ISOs)

- RTOs should work cooperatively with states on distribution-side developments to ensure that grid operations remain stable as more distributed energy is added to the grid. (Ch. 20)
- RTOs and ISOs should enact market rules to accommodate the participation of energy storage (including hydro pumped storage) in energy markets, consistent with the Federal Energy Regulatory Commission's final rule. (Ch. 22)
- RTOs and ISOs should establish new products and reform existing products that would adequately compensate ancillary services such as those provided by hydropower. (Ch. 22)
- Regional planners, which consist of transmission owners and grid operators in a specific geographical area, should consider what it would take to phase out the use of fossil-fired generation and prepare to meet long-term greenhouse gas reduction goals. (Ch. 24)

State Public Utility Commissions

- State utility commissions should adopt decoupling mechanisms so that utilities do not receive income in excess of their revenue requirement plus earned incentives, with the result that megawatt hours of sales do not drive profits. (Ch. 6)
- State utility commissions should promote a utility business model that provides new sources of revenue and profit consistent with encouraging the growth of grid-edge resources. (Ch. 6)
- State utility commissions should require measurement and verification metering and supervisory control and data acquisition devices that permit accurate measurement of energy savings and carbon performance from utility energy efficiency programs. (Ch. 6)

- State utility commissions should require utility planning that identifies locations on the utility distribution systems where location of grid edge resources can avoid the need for additional distribution assets, and should encourage utilities to engage in "utility–private partnerships" to procure services from grid-edge resources. (Ch. 6)
- Wherever a state utility commission has jurisdiction over an energy project participant, it should use its authority to require reporting of carbon performance information on an ongoing basis. (Ch. 6)
- State public utility regulatory commissions should adopt utility rate designs that align utility interests with energy efficiency, such as decoupling. (Ch. 9)
- State public utility commissions could adopt regulations to ensure that all customers receive information on the costs and benefits of switching to electricity. (Ch. 11)
- State public utility commissions should support the development of infrastructure for expanded use of electric vehicles by acting to bolster utility investment in it. (Ch. 14)
- State public utility commissions should encourage utilities to begin using grid-connected photovoltaic (solar) along with distributed battery storage to provide the benefits of resilience and emergency backup to their services. (Ch. 19)
- If state legislation is unclear regarding how to define "need" and "public use," state public utility commissions can interpret those terms expansively to encompass regional need and regional public use as well as clean energy goals within the state or the region. (Ch. 20)
- State public utility commissions could make clear that merchant transmission line companies can seek siting permits and exercise eminent domain authority under the same conditions as electric utilities. (Ch. 20)
- Utility commissions could impose a nuclear portfolio standard that would co-exist alongside existing renewable portfolio standards or broaden the scope of existing renewable portfolio standards to incorporate all "clean" energy, including nuclear power. (Ch. 21)

- State public utility commissions should direct their regulated electric utilities to evaluate the need for and benefits of grid-scale storage such as pumped storage hydro. (Ch. 22)
- State utility commissions should encourage local governments to take initiative in building clean energy infrastructure, especially to the extent that this allows them to draw on tax-free financing options. (Ch. 23)
- State public utility regulators should consider the possibility of stranded assets when assessing proposals for fossil fuel infrastructure that will be paid for by ratepayers. (Ch. 24)
- State public utility commissions should consider the possibility of stranded assets when assessing proposals for fossil fuel infrastructure that will be paid for by ratepayers, such as electric transmission lines and (in states where electric utilities are still vertically integrated) generating facilities. (Ch. 24 App. B)
- State public utility commissions should adopt renewable gas quality standards that do not operate as a barrier to pipeline transportation. (Ch. 26)
- State public utility commissions should require pipeline operators seeking to apply stricter quality standards to renewable gas than natural gas to provide a valid justification for that choice. (Ch. 26)
- State public utility commissions can help stabilize and subsidize prices for carbon capture and sequestration (CCS)-generated electricity by a variety of mechanisms, including approvals of rates to help defray the cost of CCS and power purchase agreements. (Ch. 28)